I CAN'T REMEMBER
THE TITLE BUT
THE COVER IS BLUE

STORIES FROM THE OTHER SIDE
OF THE BOOKSHOP COUNTER

I CAN'T REMEMBER THE TITLE BUT THE COVER IS BLUE

ELIAS GREIG

WITH ILLUSTRATIONS
BY PHILLIP MARSDEN

ALLEN&UNWIN
SYDNEY · MELBOURNE · AUCKLAND · LONDON

Samuel Taylor Coleridge, 'The Rime of the Ancyent Marinere' in William Wordsworth
and Samuel Taylor Coleridge, *Lyrical Ballads* (London: Longman, 1798).

John Keats, 'Ode on Indolence' 1819 in *Life, Letters, and Literary Remains of John Keats*,
ed. R.M. Milnes, vol. 2 (London: Edward Moxon, 1848).

Allen & Unwin
83 Alexander Street
Crows Nest NSW 2065
Australia
Phone: (61 2) 8425 0100
Email: info@allenandunwin.com
Web: www.allenandunwin.com

A catalogue record for this
book is available from the
NATIONAL LIBRARY OF AUSTRALIA National Library of Australia

ISBN 978 1 76052 945 1

Illustration of books: Shutterstock
All other illustrations by Phillip Marsden
Internal design by Christa Moffitt
Set in 11/18 pt Baskerville by Bookhouse, Sydney
Printed in Australia by SOS Print + Media Group

10 9 8 7

MIX
Paper from
responsible sources
FSC® C001695

The paper in this book is FSC® certified.
FSC® promotes environmentally responsible,
socially beneficial and economically viable
management of the world's forests.

To all my colleagues, comrades, and co-workers,
past and present.

There is one thing that stands out grossly to the eye, and respecting which there can be no dispute: I mean, the servile and contemptible arts which we so frequently see played off by the tradesman. He is so much in the habit of exhibiting a bended body, that he scarcely knows how to stand upright. Every word he utters is graced with a simper or a smile. He exhibits all the arts of the male coquette; not that he wishes his fair visitor to fall in love with his person, but that he may induce her to take off his goods. [. . .] There is not a being on the face of the earth, with a heart more thoroughly purged from every remnant of the weakness of benevolence and sympathy. The sole principle of all this fair outside, is the consideration how to make the most of every one that enters his shop.

Yet this being, this supple, fawning, cringing creature, this systematic, cold-hearted liar, this being, every moment of whose existence is centred in the sordid consideration of petty gains, has the audacity to call himself a man. One half of all the human beings we meet, belong, in a higher or lower degree, to the class here delineated. In how perverted a state of society have we now been destined to exist?

WILLIAM GODWIN (1756–1836),
FAILED PHILOSOPHER, FAILED BOOKSELLER

Introduction

This book, like most books, began life as a kind of therapy. After years of selling overpriced shoes, I'd gotten what I thought would be a calm, dignified job at a bookshop on Sydney's leafy, beachy North Shore. I'd just started a PhD in literature and, at last, I thought, here was a part-time job where the product I was selling was something I knew and cared about; where I might be genuinely helpful, rather than sly, enabling, and mendacious – key attributes for any worker hoping to make it in Australia's vast retail and service sector.

As any customer service worker will tell you, customers can be kind, thoughtful, funny, and full of pathos – but also irrational, demanding, intrusive, abusive, over-disclosive, and brain-scramblingly, mind-bendingly *strange*. The fraught interaction between patron and worker – the counter between us; the commercial imperative brooding above – dims down certain inhibitions and has a hothouse effect on eccentricity. To work in customer service is to be paid (hopefully) minimum wage to remain polite in the face of rudeness, to pretend all requests are welcome and reasonable, and to encourage impulsive behaviour in hope of making a sale.

All this, I thought, would be behind me. I was on my way to a better place, a place of culture and harmless entertainment, where my colleagues and I would take turns answering what I imagined as the most difficult question we'd be asked: 'I can't remember the title, but the cover is blue?' And I wasn't alone. The special place of bookshops in the popular imagination meant that many of my friends expressed something like envy: 'Oh, how lovely! I've always wanted to work in a bookshop'. Bookshops were a place of comfort, a pocket universe of humanist decency only incidentally involved in the grubby business of getting and spending.

The truth is that, far from being insulated from the absurdities of retail, bookshops seem to throw them into starker relief. Our curious position as nostalgia property, cultural dispensary, and ersatz community centre means customers feel no qualms asking for help that contradicts or has nothing to do with our status as a 'business' – from free day-care ('Just for an hour, they're no trouble') to internet research ('Thanks for the info, mate, I'll get it on Amazon'). And while all retailers encounter angst and human misery, the nature of the product means this misery is uncomfortably explicit. In the shoe shop, certain purchases hinted at midlife crisis or divorce; in the bookshop, titles like *Healing from Infidelity* leave no room for doubt. Finally, as one of the few remaining places where you can spend hours without being expected to buy anything, bookshops are the natural resort of the idle, the elderly, the lonely, the romantic, and the legitimately mad.

For my own sanity, and as a small creative outlet between part-time work and a PhD thesis, I started writing up my interactions with customers. My aim was to capture something that happened to me almost every day, to put the reader in my place, feeling my trepidation and incredulity – but also my sympathy, amusement, and delight. This book isn't or shouldn't be a simple record of misanthropy and spleen. Rather, it's a collection of weird, sometimes appalling, sometimes touching, and hopefully funny anecdotes about our bizarre historical moment: to listen to customers in a bookshop is to hear the Zeitgeist come roaring out like the Devil at an exorcism. It's a record of what the placing of a counter between people does to us, at a time when the consumer is replacing the citizen as society's basic political unit, and service culture looks set to conquer the world.

If nothing else, I hope these pieces remind readers that the person on the other side of the counter inhabits their own life just as fully. You might be curious to know what we see – particularly since what we see is you.

Elias Greig, 2018

1

Saturday, 8.50 a.m.

Buff gym-goer with a gym bag over his shoulder, sucking liquid breakfast drink through a straw, taps on the door before opening time. I let him in.

Buff Suckler: Mate, I'm switching to the iPad. It's just better.

Me: . . . Right. How can I help?

Buff Suckler: Do you do second-hand books? I've got piles of 'em – they're not in very good nick and they're probably not worth anything, but I'm looking for somewhere to dump 'em. I wouldn't want much for 'em. *pauses to slurp through straw* Would you be interested?

Me: . . . Not really, no.

Buff Suckler: *narrows eyes; suckles* Why not?

Me: . . . Well, for all the reasons you just said.

Buff Suckler: Fair enough. Do you have sex tips? *straw slurp*

BUFF SUCKLER

Me: *blinks; buffers* . . . Third row back on the left, in Sex and Relationships. I'll show you the section. *leaves counter and starts to walk to section*

Buff Suckler: Look, not to worry mate, I'll just get them on the iPad. *finishes drink, puts empty on counter, leaves*

Freckly lady in a rope necklace marches up to counter, pushes up her sunglasses, looks furious.

Me: *cautiously* Morning – how can I help?

Frecklefury: Do you have a copy of *The Secret River* by Kate Grenville?

Me: We should do – let me check . . . Yep, we do –

Frecklefury: *tight jawed* Good! I've got someone in mind for it.

Me: *fetches it from the shelf* Who are you giving it to?

Frecklefury: *with feeling* A Racist!

Me: *blinking* Oh! Awesome! Want me to gift wrap it?

Frecklefury: Would you? That'd be great.

Me: *wrapping* So . . . how do you think this person will react to the book?

Frecklefury: *snarling* I don't give a shit! *pauses; narrows eyes* I hope the bitch cries.

3

Monday, 12.15 p.m.

Jolly apple-cheeked lady customer: I love Matthew Reilly. I know it's not clever – it's heaps of fun, but.

Me: Did you like his latest?

Jolly Apple-Cheek: Yeah, but it's not for teenagers, hey.

Me: Really? Too sexy?

Jolly Apple-Cheek: Yeah, it's like about young Bess – you know, young Elizabeth – and she goes for it.

Me: *enjoys this a lot* Oh?

Jolly Apple-Cheek: And there's . . . Well, there's lots of, like, whores.

Me: Really? Whores?

Jolly Apple-Cheek: *blushes; lowers her voice conspiratorially* Yeah – you know – whores of the Early Times.

4

Monday, 10.05 a.m.

Older lady with a perm, a limp, and a big black handbag:
Hello, I know you're a bookshop, but I'm desperate to
find the Telstra store that used to be in the centre – do
you know where it went?

Me: *reluctantly* I . . . suppose I can check online for you if
you like. *light googling* Says here there's one at Warringah
Mall, so I think that's your best bet.

Old Perm: *incredulous* There isn't a closer one?

Me: *rigorous googling* No, that looks like the closest one –

Old Perm: *sharply* Are you sure?

Me: *evenly* No, but Google seems to be.

Old Perm: Thank you. *stays where she is*

Me: . . . Is there something else I can help you with?

Old Perm: Can you look up a restaurant? It's called the
European Grill. I think it's in Newtown.

Me: *suppresses a sigh* Why not? *gentle googling* It's in Newtown, on King Street –

Old Perm: *interrupts* Would you mind checking Urbanspoon? My son is taking me there for dinner.

Me: *checks Urbanspoon* It gets very good reviews.

Old Perm: *cranes around to look at the screen* Can you print this page?

Me: No.

Old Perm: . . .

Me: . . . Would you like me to write down the address?

Old Perm: Please.

5

Early Teen Customer (ETC): Do you have *Some Faults in Their Stars?*

Me: Do you mean *The Fault in Our Stars?*

ETC: Is that the one where she's got, like, cancer, but he loves her anyway?

Me: Yep, that's the one.

ETC: *eagerly* Yeah, do you have that one?

Me: We do! Did you want the regular cover, or the movie cover?

ETC: Um, the movie cover? Is that the one where you can see her cancer, like, coming out her nose?

Me: Yep.

6

Tuesday, 9.30 a.m.

Woman in pearl earrings and a purple tracksuit: Do you have a children's picture book about the Holocaust? I'm looking for something inspiring.

Me: . . . No.

Pearl Tracksuit: Have you heard of anything like that? Could you get one in?

7

Sunday, 11 a.m.

Small girl in pink swimmers repeatedly throws hardcover *Wind in the Willows* on the floor while Listless Hipster Dad watches on.

Me: *wincing as book hits floor* Everything alright?

Listless Hipster Dad: Oh yeah . . . Sorry man . . . *looks blearily at daughter* Hey Lily – don't do that, hey?

Me: *wincing as book hits floor again* Ah, maybe you could take it off her . . . ?

Listless Hipster Dad: *wryly* Parenting is hard. She's three.

Me: I believe you. *winces as book hits floor again* Do you mind if I speak to her?

Listless Hipster Dad: Sure man! *thinks for a moment* Don't yell at her, but.

Me: *gently* Lily, if you throw that book one more time, I'm going to make your daddy pay for it –

Listless Hipster Dad: LILY PUT THE BOOK DOWN RIGHT NOW!

LISTLESS HIPSTER DAD
AND LILY

8

Thursday, 10.30 a.m.

Punch-drunk mum and dreadful tennish son called Justin enter the store – Justin snivelling, punch-drunk mum clearly engaged in some kind of mindfulness practice to help with the constant horror of Justin. They head for the children's section. Dreadful Justin pulls a book roughly off the shelf, drops it on the floor, and opens it with his vile little sandalled foot.

Punch-Drunk Mum: Justin! This isn't the library! You can't just wreck things!

9

Sunday, 2 p.m.

Soberly dressed woman with bobbed blonde hair: Just this one, thanks.

Me: No worries – that's $32.99.

Sober Bob: Can I use payWave?

Me: Sure, just tap it on the side.

Sober Bob: *taps card; EFTPOS machine makes unhappy noise*

Me: *grimacing companionably* Sorry about that – our machine is pretty unfriendly –

Sober Bob: Oh, don't worry. This kind of thing happens all the time since I was struck by lightning.

Me: Wow! WOW! Really? That's fascinating!

Sober Bob: *flatly* Mm, when I was training as a nurse the ECG machines used to go haywire every time I entered the room.

Me: Extraordinary!

Sober Bob: *matter-of-factly* Yeah, there must be some residual charge.

Me: Wow! You have a dormant superpower!

Sober Bob: *ghost of a smile* Mm, well, it hasn't shown itself yet.

Me: *gathers himself* Well. You're my first-ever lightning-struck customer.

Sober Bob: Hm. We were struck as a group, my father and I, and some others – not all of us made it.

Me: Oh. *sombre pause* Well. One of my colleagues has the dubious honour of having been attacked by a shark –

Sober Bob: *quietly amused* Mm, that happened to me, too. I don't usually tell that to people, though – it seems ridiculous on top of the lightning.

14

10

Monday, 9.05 a.m.

Salt-and-pepper builder beard, trailed, at a safe distance, by mute apprentice: Mate, do you sell electrical extension leads?

Me: No. No, definitely not.

Builder Beard: *looks angrily from me to mute apprentice and back in search of conspiracy*

Me: *foolishly attempts to defuse tension over predictable lack of leads with limp joke* We might have a book on electrical extension leads . . . ?

Builder Beard: *puts a paint-flecked finger in my face* There's no need to be smart, mate! *stalks out*

Mute Apprentice: *looks stricken; silently counts to ten; scurries after him*

11

Saturday, 10.45 a.m.

Woman who looks remarkably like a corella: Yehs.

Me: **blinks** Yes?

Corella Woman: Yehs. I need a book of nibbles for my grand-nephew – he's got five of them but his grandmother wants him to have more.

Me: **translation software; memory palace** So the *Aussie Nibbles* early readers?

Corella Woman: Yehs.

Me: **reflexively** Yes. Ah, yes, we have them – do you know which five he's read?

Corella Woman: No. How many of them are there?

Me: How many *Aussie Nibbles*?

Corella Woman: Yehs.

Me: Heaps. Shall I show you where they are?

CORELLA WOMAN

Corella Woman: Yehs. *pauses; thinks* But how will I know which ones he already has?

Me: I'm not sure. Could you get in touch with his grandmother?

Corella Woman: No. She won't know. Do you know?

Me: Do I know which five *Aussie Nibbles* your grand-nephew has read?

Corella Woman: Yehs.

Me: No.

Corella Woman: Oh.

12

Saturday, 2.30 p.m.

Brisk lady with a high blonde ponytail and a maddeningly fussy start-stop way of speaking: Hi. I'll take this. *drops luridly pink children's book on counter*

Me: Sure –

High Pony Start-Stop: Actually. It's a gift. Would you mind wrapping it for me?

Me: No worries –

High Pony Start-Stop: Actually. Would you mind? I've got a few more. I didn't buy them here. Could you wrap them up with it? *drops two more pinky-purple books on counter; winces a smile*

Me: *cheerfully* Sure –

High Pony Start-Stop: What colours do you have?

Me: In the paper? We've got a few . . . *ducks behind counter to bring out rolls of gift wrap*

High Pony Start-Stop: *leans over counter* Do you have pink?

Me: *head in paper draw* Yep. *surfaces* It looks like this.

High Pony Start-Stop: *sharply* And? What else?

Me: Green, orange, and a sort of silvery black –

High Pony Start-Stop: Actually. Would you mind doing all three in different colours? One pink, one green, and one black?

Me: *bland smile* Sure –

High Pony Start-Stop: And then just wrap one ribbon around all three?

Me: Sure –

High Pony Start-Stop: What kind of ribbon do you have?

Me: . . . We've got a few different colours . . .

High Pony Start-Stop: *raises eyebrows* Can I see them?

Me: Sure – any particular colour you're after?

High Pony Start-Stop: *incredulously* Um . . . ? I won't know until I see them?

Me: Right. *manages not to grind teeth* Well . . . *makes a small pile of different ribbons on counter*

High Pony Start-Stop: Wow. You've got heaps.

Me: We do. So – *heartily* which one?

High Pony Start-Stop: Oh. God. I'm not sure now. Pick one for me.

Me: . . . Ah – what about this one? *holds up stripy ribbon*

High Pony Start-Stop: *sharply* Yep. Looks good.

Me: *begins to wrap presents*

High Pony Start-Stop: Actually.

Me: *wide-eyed, edging towards hysteria* The colour no good?

High Pony Start-Stop: No. The colour's fine. But can you do me a gift receipt, just in case they need to return it? It's a gift, so . . . ?

Me: Of course – one second. *writes gift receipt, slips inside front cover, and recommences wrapping*

High Pony Start-Stop: . . . Actually.

Me: *alarmed, wide-eyed, quiet breath out, still wrapping* Was there anything else . . . ?

High Pony Start-Stop: *writhes closed lips* Nope. I can't think of anything else to ask you for. *ghostly smile*

Me: *still wrapping; manages a kindly smile* Getting your money's worth, eh?

High Pony Start-Stop: *with passion* Oh, absolutely! The minimum wage in this country is ridiculous. It's completely over the top!

Me: Oh. *measures out ribbon; cuts* Well. *evens and loops ribbon* I hope I'm justifying my wage.

High Pony Start-Stop: *steely smile, pointed eye contact* We'll see in a minute.

Me: *ties ribbon in a bow, smooths, cuts rough edges* There we go – how's that?

High Pony Start-Stop: Perfect. Looks great.

Me: Thanks. So, that's $12.95

High Pony Start-Stop: *sharply* Is it? How much was the wrapping?

Me: The wrapping was free.

High Pony Start-Stop: *Huskily, and with deep satisfaction* Good.

13

Monday, 4.15 p.m.

Hairless man with very prominent teeth and a pronounced sibilance in his speech: Exsscuse me – do you have Bram Sstoker'ss *Dracula* in the Oxford World'ss Classsicss edition?

Me: *delighted* Yes!

14

Sunday, 3.20 p.m.

Gaggle of unaccompanied children enter store and swarm into the children's section. One small boy, probably two or three years old, strains for a large animal encyclopedia just out of reach until his sister (four or five) hands it down to him. He hefts it, throws it flat on the carpet and begins to jump on it. Swooping in to rescue the book, I reel back, eyes watering from the ripe, rich aroma wafting from the jumping child.

Me: *to sister* Is this little guy your brother?

Sister: Yes.

Me: *blinking through the stench* I think you better take him to find your parents.

Sister: Why?

Me: I think he's filled his nappy.

Sister: *surprisingly hearty snigger* He's not wearing a nappy!

15

Monday, 5 p.m.

Sporty older lady customer in gym shoes, lycra, and a pink hoodie: Aw, hi! *scrunches up face, snaps fingers* Aw! What was it? I just saw it . . .

Me: *encouraging midwife smile* Was it a book? What kind of book?

Pink Hoodie: Yeah – yeah. A crime book – can't remember the name . . .

Me: A new book? Maybe by a foreign author?

Pink Hoodie: YES! A foreign author . . . Aaaawww, what was it?

Me: Jo Nesbo? Henning Mankell? Andrea Camilleri? Stieg Larsson?

Pink Hoodie: You know, I just can't remember. Isn't that terrible? I just saw it . . .

Me: What did the cover look like? Was it a new release? Or something you've been after for a while?

Pink Hoodie: I think it was a bit white with some black and red writing. God, I only just saw it!

Me: Where did you see it?

Pink Hoodie: Well, I saw it in the paper . . . and in town, and in a bigger shop, I think it was Myer? You've definitely got it.

Me: We might do, yeah. Is it [new title]? Or [slightly older title]?

Pink Hoodie: No, no, none of those.

Me: What about [etc]?

Pink Hoodie: Nup.

Me: *apologetically* I'm not sure . . . with a bit more info, I'm sure we can track it down, but I'm not sure we've got it.

Pink Hoodie: *impatiently* Look, I know you've got it.

Me: *bemused* How do you know?

Pink Hoodie: Because it's in your window! *nasal sigh*

Me: . . .

Pink Hoodie: . . .

Me: . . .

Pink Hoodie: Can you get it?

Me: . . . Yes.

16

Sunday, 1.15 p.m.

European man in orange jeans: Hhello, I bhought a bhook here rhecently, it was call *Zhe'ro Wauhn T-hoo*, by Pehter Zhiel – hit's habout starrt-hup bisnehs. Do you have a nohther wauhn?

Me: *vigorous computer searching* Right . . . Is it *Zero to One*, by Peter Thiel?

Orange Jeans: Yhes, ehxacktly!

Me: We should have it – it's in the Business and Finance section. *walks to section, followed eagerly by Orange Jeans* So it should be here, give me a second. *squats on heels, scans bottom shelf*

Orange Jeans: *stands uncomfortably close; orange crotch eclipses half my vision* Khan you see hit?

Me: *eyes front, orange crotch blazing in peripheral vision* It should be here – just, ah, give me a minute –

Orange Jeans: Zher! Zher it is! *crowds in further; points with toe*

Me: *closes one eye against crotch glare, relieved* Well spotted –

Orange Jeans: Yhou haf t-hoo poosh for what yhou whant – it's what zhe bhook teaches! *minute pelvic thrust*

Me: *recoils; stands up very quickly*

17

Saturday, 11 a.m.

Infectiously peppy primary teacher: Hi! I have a book to pick up! *Indian in the Cupboard*?

Me: One sec . . . Yep, here it is. I remember loving this as a kid.

Infectious Pep: Me too! I'm reading it with my class!

Me: *catches the pep* Cool! I'm sure they'll love it.

Infectious Pep: Yeah! Though I'm leaving out one bit.

Me: Oh? Which bit?

Infectious Pep: You know, the part where they become blood brothers.

Me: *chuckles* I can see how you wouldn't want that to catch on in the playground!

Infectious Pep: *leans in with bulging eyes* I KNOW! I mean, HELLO! AIDS!

18

Monday, 2.50 p.m.

Lady in sun visor: Yes, I'm after a book . . . I can't remember the title, but it's quite unique . . .

Me: Do you remember what it's about?

Sun Visor: It's about a French woman, and she finally tells her story. Do you have that one?

19

Righteous magpie lady and her drooping, sweetly bespectacled son approach the counter. Bespectacled son puts a lavish new cookbook from Yotam Ottolenghi on the counter.

Sweet Specs: He-ey . . . Can we have this one? And can we, um, get it gift-wrapped?

Me: Sure. This is a great cookbook! *scans it* I'll just wrap it for you – is it for a man, or a woman, or doesn't matter?

Sweet Specs: Uhh –

Righteous Magpie Lady: *swoops in* Why does THAT matter?! Why are you asking that?

Me: *winces; holds up hands* I know, I know! It's just people are sometimes particular –

Righteous Magpie Lady: Well, I don't see why you should PANDER to them!

Me: *wincing even more* No, no – I know –

Righteous Magpie Lady: I mean, you're just wrapping a present! Why would you . . . ? *waves hands violently, trying to think of the deeply iniquitous, patriarchy-high-fiving thing I'm doing*

Me: *still wincing; helplessly finishes her sentence* . . . Why would I reinforce strict gender binaries?

Righteous Magpie Lady: Exactly! Why would you do that?

Me: *making self small* It's just that people have asked me to re-wrap things if they think they're not feminine enough, or vice versa – I know it's a fig-leaf, but that's why I throw in that third option –

Righteous Magpie Lady: That's ridiculous! Why would you give in to that sort of thing?

Me: *writhes* Pandering is sort of part of my job . . . *trails off dejectedly*

Righteous Magpie Lady: *obviously disgusted* Well, this book is for a MAN! But I don't want MASCULINE wrapping!

Me: No, no, of course! *takes a deep breath* How's purple?

Righteous Magpie Lady: Purple is fine!

Me: *wraps present with shaking hands*

RIGHTEOUS MAGPIE LADY AND SWEET SPECS

20

Sunday, 3.30 p.m.

Muscular father and son duo, both tanned and wearing grey singlets, enter store with sense of purpose, scoop up and pass from hand to hand a copy of Cheryl Strayed's *Wild*. At Muscular Son's urging, Muscular Father places book on counter and gestures brawnily at it.

Muscular Father: That one, mate.

Me: *tight-jawed approval* Great book. *blokey nod and smile-frown*

Muscular Father: *hands over money*

Me: Did you see the movie?

Muscular Father: Nah. Any good?

Me: *more blokey nodding* Great film. You should go.

Muscular Father: *twists mouth; pained expression* Yeah, but it's got whatzername in it, doesn't it?

Me: Reese Witherspoon?

Muscular Father: Yeah, see, she doesn't do anything for me – physically – and I can't be bothered watching anyone I'm not attracted to for that long. She just doesn't do it for me. *thinks for a moment; faraway Hemingway look* Bit like Meryl Streep.

Me: . . .

Muscular Son: *wordlessly pushes Muscular Father – hard – out of the way, picks up book and meets my eye, smiling desperately* Is it a good book?

Me: *Equally desperate smile* It's fantastic –

Muscular Son: Awesome! *gives absurd thumbs up*

Me: Enjoy it! *absurdly returns thumbs up*

21
Sunday, 10.05 a.m.

Disputatious couple enter store arguing steadily at medium volume. As they pass counter, both pause to say hello – the woman tight-lipped but polite; the man with a shaved head and brain-scrambling, toe-curling halitosis. They stop in the children's section and argue about which book to get for a friend's child.

Tight-Lip: We could get *The Gruffalo* but they've probably already got it but it's really a good one and kids like it and I don't know what else to get and how much should we spend?

Halitosis: *makes mooing noises; loses interest; drifts away across the shop leaving a skunk-trail of mouth smells*

Tight-Lip: *still talking* Do you reckon they'll care if they've already got it? Todd? Todd? *realises Halitosis has drifted away* Todd! Where are you? Where did he go?

Me: *from behind the counter* He's in the travel section.

Tight-Lip: *exasperated* How do you know where he is and I don't?

Me: [I can smell him I can smell him I can smell him I can smell him I can smell him I CAN SMELL HIM] I can see over the shelves. *gestures at height*

22

Sunday, 11.40 a.m.

Curly-haired sarong lady fresh from the beach enters shop with sense of purpose; strides into the fiction section. Emerges moments later with growing urgency, interrupts my conversation with another customer.

Curly Purpose: I can't find N –

Me: *distractedly* Hold on one second for me – *finishes up with other customer* How can I help?

Curly Purpose: I can't find N!

Me: *thinks very hard; skips many questions* So which book were you after?

Curly Purpose: *Suite Française* –

Me: I know it. *checks computer* We've got it – it's by Irène Némirovsky –

Curly Purpose: *becoming exasperated* I know who it's by, I can't find –

Me: You can't find N – ahhh, I see. Fiction is over here. *leads the way*

Curly Purpose: Yeah! *walks with me* I got up to M, but I couldn't find where N began – where do you start N?

Me: *awed silence*

MIGHT BE ROB PALMER

23

Saturday, 10.15 a.m.

Blokey, curly, surfer dude who might be Rob Palmer, host of various outdoor shows: Mate, do you have . . . *reads from his iPhone* Ma-DAM Bo-VAR-ee, by Goose-TEV Flow-BERT and . . . *reads from iPhone* There-EEZ Rak-win by AY-meal Zol-uh?

Me: Yep.

Might Be Rob Palmer: Aw, good. They're for my wife.

24

Tuesday, 2.20 p.m.

Richly dressed, clearly miserable woman, followed at a distance by two surly, teary-eyed children under the age of eight, peers at me through her despairing fringe like a driver through heavy rain.

Misery Fringe: Do you keep Rachel Cusk?

Me: *blinks carefully* Yes. Yes we do. *knows the answer, but asks anyway* Which one of her books were you after?

Misery Fringe: The one about divorce.

Me: *blinks even more carefully* Sure. I'll check.

25

Sprightly lady with a swishy haircut and a cheerful air of competence: Hello! I'm looking for a dreadful book about a criminal.

My Colleague Arthur (MCA): *enjoys this a lot* We've got lots of those – was there one in particular you wanted?

Sprightly Swish: Yes, actually – it's called *Mayhem*. It's about Christopher Binse, the bank robber.

MCA: I'll check.

Me: *has sudden Sherlock Holmes flash of dropping a whole pile of this book while shelving* We've got it – one sec.

MCA: *making conversation while I return with book* So why this one in particular?

Sprightly Swish: *beams* Well, I used to work in a bank, and he held me up.

Me and MCA: *Really?*

Sprightly Swish: Oh yes – he put a shotgun in my face.

Me and MCA: *mutual goggling, wowing, etc.*

Me: *flourishes cover of book with picture of Christopher 'Badne$$' Binse on it* So is, ah, this the book you wanted? *mock gravity* Do you recognise this man?

Sprightly Swish: *brightly* That's Christopher! I recognise him there. At the trial he threw me off by shaving his head – took me a while to be sure, but you don't forget. It's funny now, but I was terrified for years afterwards – took a long time to get over.

Me: ...

MCA: ...

Me: ... Well. I don't think we've ever had a victim of the subject of a crime book in before – I'm not sure what the procedure is. But, I think we should give you some kind of discount.

Sprightly Swish: *beams again* Oh! Thank you very much!

26

Cheerful British chappie whom I've suspected as a Neo-Nazi since he ordered *Mein Kampf* last year: Hullo! I'm lookin' for a coupl'a books – I don't have *all* the information, but you've never let me down yet. *twinkles charmingly*

Me: *with very mixed feelings* Sure – what are the books?

Cheerful Possible Nazi: So, first one – I doubt you'll have it – the author's surname is Wessels. Keywords: Rhodesia; SAS; defence.

Me: *moves needle of Neo-Nazi gauge to 'very possible'* Sure. Let me check. *googles and discovers book in question, a boy's own account of the Rhodesian SAS's counterinsurgency with the (perhaps) accidentally erotic title of* A Handful of Hard Men – *not available in Australia** So the book is called *A Handful of Hard Men*, but I can't get it in, I'm afraid – it's not available in Australia. *quietly relieved*

Cheerful Very Possible Nazi: *winces cartoonishly in a completely charming and non-Nazi way* No worries, mate, no worries. Actually, would you mind writing down the details for me?

Me: *queasily* Sure. *enables the Very Possible Nazi*

Cheerful Very Possible Nazi: Cheers, mate, I really appreciate your service.

Me: *swallows* No worries. What was the second book?

Cheerful Very Possible Nazi: *thinks* . . . All I've got, and it's not much, is a subject – Brexit – and a Christian name: Arron. Sorry, mate, I know that's not much. *smiles apologetically and not at all like a Nazi*

Me: *moves needle of Neo-Nazi gauge to 'probable'* Is it *The Bad Boys of Brexit* by Arron Banks?

Cheerful Probable Nazi: *groans appreciatively* That's it – brilliant – do you have it?

Me: No, but *accommodates the Probable Nazi* we can get it in for you. *hates himself*

Cheerful Probable Nazi: Would you? That'd be really kind.

Me: *is really kind to the Probable Nazi and orders his book about Brexit*

Cheerful Probable Nazi: Tell you what, mate, do you mind if I leave you to finish that? I'll be back in a bit for something to read now once I've had me 'air cut.

I wave him out blithely, feeling stricken, and review Probable Nazi's ordering history, which begins, ominously, with *Mein Kampf*, takes in a number of non-fictional accounts of counter-insurgency practised by uniformly heroic white colonials against various colonised peoples, and concludes, in a chillingly banal flourish, with Steve Coogan's mock autobiography of Alan Partridge. I share my anxieties with my colleagues, one of whom sensibly reminds me that people have a historical interest in *Mein Kampf*, and don't need to be Nazis to be curious, which mollifies me slightly. Neo-Nazi-gauge drops one level. I resume calling customers about special orders.

Cheerful Very Possible Nazi re-enters store and, mercifully, puts a perfectly normal thriller on the counter.

Cheerful Very Possible Nazi: Thanks again for your help, mate! I'll take this one to tide me over.

Me: *beams because the nice man seems less like a Nazi* No worries!

Cheerful Very Possible Nazi: *notices a Robert Harris thriller next to the till, one of the special orders I've been calling through* Actually, mate – hang on a sec. *points at the Robert Harris thriller* Can you check to see if you 'ave another one of his books?

Me: *tenses* Which one?

Cheerful Very Possible Nazi: I think it's called *Fatherland*.

Me: *numbly checks computer* No, we don't . . . *despairing; sick at heart* Do you . . . want me to get it in for you?

27

Older lady customer, coiffured beehive, tasteful twin-set, pearls, marvellous elocution: Do you have an autobiography of Doris Day?

Me: *delighted* Yes!

28

Tuesday, 11 a.m.

Somnambulant mother and initially cute four-year-old boy approach. Somnambumum puts down a pile of books on counter; four year old stretches up to hand a crumby activity book to me directly.

Somnambumum: *tiredly* Baxter, I said you couldn't have that one. *takes book from out of my hand*

Me: *smiling indulgently* Nice try, Baxter – very cunning.

Somnambumum returns book to children's section; returns to counter. Baxter slouches towards children's section and returns with same book; attempts to hand it to me.

Somnambumum: Baxter. No, I said. *takes book; returns it to shelf*

Cycle repeats.

Somnambumum: Baxter! No!

SOMNAMBUMUM
AND BAXTER

Baxter: *deploys calculated smile – pushes book towards me*

Me: *takes book, puts it behind counter, smirks triumphantly*
Checkmate, Baxter!

Baxter: *howls*

29

Superbusy ninja mum who really doesn't need any extra frippery just quick service, thanks: I'm hoping you can help me.

Me: *affably* Me too!

Superbusy Service Thanks: *annoyed by this little bit of whimsy all in her face like a blowfly* Can you track down a copy of *says it very slowly* Waiting. For. Godot. by Samuel Beckett for my son?

Me: *bulging with mirth at the excellent joke he is about to make* Well, I'll certainly *try*! As long as you don't mind . . . *waiting*!

Superbusy Service Thanks: . . .

Me: *deflates* We've got it – I'll get it.

30

Monday, 3 p.m.

Me: *calling the United Book Distributors claims department*

Jan at UBD claims department: *with lunch lady levels of weariness and bile* United Book Distributors, this is Jan.

Me: Hi, Jan – it's Elias from North Shore Books – how are you?

Jan at UBD: *suddenly flirtatious* Oh, it's E-liiiiiiiii-as . . .

Me: *small, Dr Hibbert-ish laugh* Yes. It is.

Jan at UBD: *suggestively* We like it when *you* call, E-liiiiiii-as – you've got a lovely deep voice.

Me: *blushes* Oh, that's kind of you to say – I'm much less attractive in person.

Jan at UBD: *with unimaginable sleaze* Oh, that doesn't really matter to us, Eeeeeelllliiiiias – we don't care what you look like.

Me: *giggles shrilly*

31

The saddest woman in the whole world, apropos of nothing at all: I don't suppose there is such a thing as the perfect card for a very sad 99-year-old woman in a nursing home who has trouble with her eyes, is there?

Me: *gazes across that sunless sea* . . . No, I don't suppose there is. There are some things that cards can't do.

Saddest Woman in the Whole World: I've been looking for two months and I can't seem to find just the right thing to cheer her up. She's very sad and I want to get her just the right card. I thought it might be the one with the little black cat – the pop-up one – but now I'm not sure . . . What do you think?

Me: *hears the curfew knell of parting day* I think that it would be very difficult to find a card to make her feel better, especially if she doesn't see very well.

Saddest Woman in the Whole World: I used to get her musical cards. I got her one about the queen and you opened it and, you know, there was that music . . .

Me: *feels the darkness build behind the sky* Well, I guess it's a good idea to appeal to the senses she still has – if she hears well, then music is a good idea. *tentatively* But perhaps you shouldn't be too hard on yourself if you can't find the right card for her?

Saddest Woman in the Whole World: I should probably give up, but I love coming in here and looking at all your cards! All the different colours and everything – oh, it just takes me away! I come in every week – you've probably seen me.

Me: *walking back to the counter in full graveyard-school melancholy* You're always welcome.

Saddest Woman in the Whole World: *suddenly anxious* I do buy them – I'm always buying them, don't worry! I'm sure it's okay if I come in here and look at them if I sometimes buy them, isn't it?

Me: *utterly stricken* Of course you can! You don't need to buy them – you can come in here whenever you like!

Saddest Woman in the Whole World: *still anxious* I buy a lot of your cards – I love your cards. I love looking at them. I better go now, I suppose. Thank you for your help! *trails nervously out of the store*

Me: *calling after* Please don't feel shy! You can look at the cards! You're always allowed to look at the cards!

'THE HIMALAYAS'

32

Sunday, 1 p.m.

Compact man wearing a rope bracelet and a T-shirt reading 'The Himalayas' approaches the counter with (despite his canvas shorts) a mystic, priestly air, like Varys at the laundromat.

'The Himalayas': Hello.

Me: Hello.

'The Himalayas': *clasps hands* Do you have a book of poetry by Yoko Ono called *Acorn?*

Me: *clasps hands; unclasps hands to type* We don't, I'm afraid. Sorry about that. Would you like me to order it in for you?

'The Himalayas': *actually puts a finger to his lips* No. *thinks* Do you have any books by the artist Leunig?

Me: *nods sagely* We do. Let me show you the way.

33

Monday, 2.05 p.m.

Middle-aged country lady wearing a sequinned T-shirt with a bird on it: Do you have any little love books?

Me: *buffers* Like gift books?

Country Birdshirt: Yeah, like little books with love in 'em. I'm from the country.

Me: *enjoys this* I see. We do! I'll show you where they are. *walks her to the section*

Country Birdshirt: *makes sour face* Is this all the love books you have?

Me: Yep, I think so. None of these what you're after?

Country Birdshirt: *sucks teeth* Nup. What about books with animals in 'em?

Me: Gift books again? Or books about animals?

Country Birdshirt: Nah, like books with pictures of animals and kinky quotes.

Me: *rocketing eyebrows, blinking, etc.* Kinky quotes?

Country Birdshirt: Yeah, like one page has a duckling on it and says something nice about mums.

Me: Oh, right! *vigorous, relieved nodding* Like affirmational quotes?

Country Birdshirt: Yeah, cute ones.

34

Designer stubble in suit and tie (cologne strength = real estate agent) powerstrides up to the counter and drops *The Libertarian Alternative* on it with an excess of shoulder and chin.

Stubbletarian: How much is that?

Me: $29.99.

Stubbletarian: *sniffs dismissively; pulls an enraging face* That much?

Me: *tumbleweed blows across empty heart* That much.

Stubbletarian: *wrestles with his billfold for custody of his Amex; notices a gift book of luridly idiotic Trump quotes* Ha! How funny is this guy? Do you sell many of these?

Me: A few.

Stubbletarian: *still looking at Trump book* People that stupid shouldn't be allowed to vote. *flares his nostrils appreciatively at the whiff of his own brand*

Me: So, Amex? *slides EFTPOS terminal forward pointedly* Tap on the side or chip in the top.

Stubbletarian: *hovers card uncertainly over terminal*

Me: Tap on the side *taps side of terminal with index finger* or chip in the top. *mimes inserting card*

Stubbletarian: *taps card on top; nothing happens*

Me: So, tap on the *side* *taps the side* or chip in the *top*. *mimes*

Stubbletarian: *waves card uncertainly over the diagonal – terminal responds with text instructing closer contact – then rests card on top of the terminal; nothing happens*

Me: *more cheerful by the second* So, this time for sure – tap on the *siiiiiide* *rubs the side in circular motion* or Chip. In. The. Top. *jauntily punctuates each word with a mimed insert action*

Stubbletarian: *moves in to tap the card on top*

Me: *spins terminal at the last moment so side faces up; payment accepted* There we go! *beams*

Stubbletarian: Thanks, mate. *ruffled; eyes the machine* Is that a new machine or something?

Me: Nope. Do you need a bag?

35

Wednesday, 4.15 p.m.

Fancily dressed older woman in heavy pewter eye shadow fussily gestures for my attention from the other end of the counter: Excuse me? Excuse me! *holds up fatuous, glittery card with a picture of the Eiffel Tower and 'PARIS MON AMIE' in big red letters on it* I wonder – can you translate the text for me?

Me: *with heroic restraint* I can – it says, 'Paris my friend'.

Fancy Paris: Oh, 'my friend', thank you. Do you speak French?

Me: *startled* Ah, no, not at all.

Fancy Paris: *suspiciously* Well, how did you know what it said so quickly? I thought you'd have to look it up.

Me: *self-effacing smile* I've just heard the expression before somewhere.

Fancy Paris: *sharply* Where did you hear it? Have you been to France?

Me: *laughs* No, no, never – I can't remember where I first heard it.

Fancy Paris: *grudgingly* Well, I'm very impressed.

36

Saturday, 10.30 a.m.

Rumplemum and Fleecedaughter walk nervously up to the counter.

Rumplemum: Hi. We, um, we have a voucher . . . *fidgets*

Me: *smiles encouragingly* Great!

Rumplemum: We've got a voucher but, ah, but the dog – *scrunches up her face apologetically* the dog chewed it up. *hunts in purse, extracts gladbag with mauled voucher inside* She chews everything. Can we still use it?

Me: *squints through the murky plastic* Yep – as long as we can still read the numbers, it's fine.

Rumplemum: Do you want me to take it out of the bag?

Me: No, I think it can stay in there.

37

Monday, 11.50 a.m.

Intense lady wearing two kinds of stripes puts both hands on the counter; leans a long way in.

Me: *leans back* Hi there!

Two Kinds of Stripes: *fervidly maintains eye contact*

Me: *blinks benignly* How can I help?

Two Kinds of Stripes: My daughter is starting university and she needs a great deal of help and protection.

Me: Right. So. *clasps hands in front of himself to establish personal space* Academic help? Or more personal help?

Two Kinds of Stripes: Both. I'm hoping you have some cards.

Me: *brain crash; switches to emergency question-repeat mode* Some cards?

Two Kinds of Stripes: Yes, the *Law of Attraction* cards by Esther Hicks.

Me: *hard reset; customer service software reboot* I'll check . . . We don't have any in stock, but I can certainly get some in for you if you'd like.

Two Kinds of Stripes: Could you? How soon? It's desperately urgent.

38

Stiff, puny kid in his late teens with a neatly trimmed chin beard approaches counter, accompanied by his comb-over father in clear aviators and a nylon racing team polo shirt finished with a thin gold chain.

Stiffchin Punybeard: *in the clipped, arctic tones of the social-climbing poisoner* Yes, good afternoon. I believe a book I ordered has arrived: *The Road to Serfdom* by Friedrich Hayek.

Me: *smiles his warmest, widest, welfare-state smile* Is that right? What name was it under?

Stiffchin Punybeard: It's B—

Me: Yep, here it is.

Stiffchin Punybeard: *licks dry lips; eyes blaze with the dry fire of fanatical pleasure* Good.

This was the day I could have stopped Voldemort.

39
Saturday, 12.15 p.m.

Very old lady in floral shirt with a prophetic eye fixes me with an Ancient Mariner stare as she makes her way slowly into the store.

Floral Prophet: I hear them talking. *pauses dramatically*

Me: *listens like a three years' child – the mariner hath her will*

Floral Prophet: I hear them talking . . . on the radio.

Me: . . . Oh. And what *optimistically adjusts the tense* were they talking about?

Floral Prophet: *peers into the mysteries of the universe* Children's books. What are they talking about?

Me: *achieves lucidity with great mental effort* Are you looking for a children's book? For a gift? How old is the child?

Floral Prophet: What would they be talking about? Which writers of children's stories would they be talking about on the radio? What is there?

Me: *fights the hypnotic power of the Floral Prophet's stare* Well, I can recommend all kinds of things, but who are you shopping for?

Floral Prophet: *deeply puzzled* What do you mean?

Me: *suddenly unsure about meaning in general* Ah, is there a child you are shopping for?

Floral Prophet: *muses upon this* I just want to know which notable authors of children's stories might be featured on the radio.

Me: *closes eyes very tightly; blinks; breathes* Well, I can show you some that might have been featured in the past. Were you thinking picture books or chapter books?

Floral Prophet: *portentously* Nothing ... specific ... I just want ... a general idea. They speak about it on the radio often.

Me: *increasingly desperate* Who does? Were you listening to the ABC? Was it 702?

Floral Prophet: *becoming annoyed* Just show me some children's books they might mention on the radio.

74

FLORAL PROPHET

Me: *reaches out blindly; grabs* Pig the Pug* This book has been very popular.

Floral Prophet: *peers at it intensely*

Phone rings.

Me: Will you excuse me for a moment? I just have to grab that phone. *flees*

40

Sunday, 10.15 a.m.

Smoky lady customer in a pink tracksuit: Excuse me – I can't
remember the author, but they printed a bit of it in the
The Daily Telegraph – do you have the book about prisons
where the man from *Hey Dad!* has shit thrown on him in
jail for being a paedophile?

Me: Yep.

41

The day after the Sydney siege, modestly dressed woman in classic Jennifer Byrnewear who turns out to be the worst approaches the counter with an air of condescending tolerance, as if I were blowing raspberries and she were ignoring it.

Worst Byrne: Hi – I'm wondering – *sighs* – I'm interested in a few of these tote bags. *disgruntled pause*

Me: Sure! Which tote bags?

Worst Byrne: *as if I were peeing on her foot* These. *points at wooden rack of tote bags in plastic wrap, secured to rack with cable ties* But, uh, how can I buy them if they're attached to this rack? *means, in her mind, 'Why are you such a revolting piece of human flotsam?'*

Me: *grins like a golden retriever* Ah, yes! They're very secure, aren't they? Luckily, I have scissors. *flourishes scissors like a plump magician*

Worst Byrne: Why are they attached in a way that means I can't buy them? *means, in her mind, 'How did you learn to walk upright, and who taught you human speech?'*

Me: *chuckles heartily* It's a little trap we set so customers have to talk to us. *snips required cable ties and hands over tote bags*

Worst Byrne: *Seriously?*

Me: *drops any pretence of good cheer* No, not seriously. I'd say we had to attach them to the rack and maybe we were feeling a little paranoid about theft – I'm not sure.

Worst Byrne: *wrinkles nostrils as if I had produced a smell; sighs with soul-deep weariness and exasperation* I think we have better things to be paranoid about now, don't you?

Me: *blinded by this flash of perspective; staggered that a mortal could speak such potent, lofty truths* So, was it just the two bags, then?

42

Fat-cheeked boy with face graze slams a Lego book on the counter.

Fat-Cheeked Facegraze: I get to go to Darren's party! I got an invitation and it said that I'm invited!

Me: Great! How exciting! Will there be cake?

Fat-Cheeked Facegraze: *draws in deep breath, eyes wide in rapture* YES THERE WILL BE CAAAAKE! IT'S THE BEST PAAART!

43

Porcine chappy in blue polo shirt and silver chain enters store while on the phone and plants one elbow on the counter.

Pork Chap: *on the phone* Yep . . . Yep . . . right. Mate! Can I borrow a pen and paper?

Me: *wordlessly slides over pen and Post-it*

Pork Chap: *on phone* Yep . . . So what's it called? *licks lips* Right. *writes a book title on Post-it; signs off and pockets phone; points pen at Post-it*

Me: . . .

Pork Chap: *looks at me expectantly* Got that? *taps Post-it with pen*

Me: *flatly* I'll check. Finished with the pen?

Pork Chap: Yep. *hands it back; sudden pained expression crosses piggy face* Actually, can I have it back for a sec? I've got, *takes pen* aw, a really bad, *twists hand holding pen behind back* aw, itch! *scratches self vigorously with back of pen, breathes out, settles back into polo shirt* That's better.

44

Tuesday, 3.15 p.m.

Elegantly dressed woman with an air of baroque, Continental gloom: Will I find anything in here that would interest my grandfather?

Me: *hears the sad viola music of the Old World* I, ah, hope so – what's he usually interested in?

Continental Gloom: Hmmm . . . *wanders over to fiction section*

Me: *follows uncertainly* Would you like some suggestions?

Continental Gloom: *contemplative silence* Will he like a book?

Me: *struck dumb with melancholy, as if alone on some winter street under cold stars framed by bare branches*

Continental Gloom: Perhaps this one . . . ? *wafts a novel off the shelf, looks vaguely at it*

Me: . . . Yes. *approaching fugue state*

Continental Gloom: Will I buy him a card?

This is the bookshop of J. Alfred Prufrock.

45

Saturday, 4.40 p.m.

Tanned louche with designer salt-and-pepper stubble, and a pair of Ray-Bans pulling his collar down to show more of himself, puts two expensive coffee table books on the counter – one about Venice, the other a collection of fifty years of Pirelli calendar babes.

Tanned Louche: *lavishly; with much too much tongue* This shop is amazing. It's filled with beautiful things.

Me: *smiles blankly; scans books*

Tanned Louche: Have you *seen* this one? *strokes and admires the Venice book obscenely* I l-u-u-u-h-v Venice.

Me: *smiles blankly; bags Venice*

Tanned Louche: And *this* book *takes the Pirelli book lovingly into his arms; half-opens it to show a hint of classy boob* is stunning. I *love *pauses; thinks* Pirelli.

Me: *smiles blankly* $250, please.

TANNED LOUCHE

46

Sunday, 11 a.m.

Porcupine lady, pink lipstick, purple hair: Sweetheart, can you wrap this one for me? It's for my mother.

Me: Sure! *wrapping; selects brown ribbon to match purple paper; begins to tie bow*

Pink and Purple Porcupine: Honey, stop riiiight there.

Me: *stops right there*

Pink and Purple Porcupine: Do you have a different colour ribbon?

Me: Of course – you don't like the brown?

Pink and Purple Porcupine: Darling, it is *such* a sleazy brown.

47

Mologuing pashmina woman with consciously international accent: Hello I need a bhook for my daughter she had a chald last year and I'm looking for something with Australian animals in it suitable for a two-year-old girl something not too heavy I can post –

Me: *smiles; already weary*

International Pashmina: Is this section the section for children's books with Australian animals in them? I don't whant anything too complicated she's still a chald and her mother is –

Me: *hands over a series of conspicuously Australian children's books, including* Possum Magic, Wombat Stew, Diary of a Wombat, *etc., etc.*

International Pashmina: *still talking* I'm not su-ure about whombats – they've never seen a whombat and – OH!

Me: *starts* Oh?

International Pashmina: *points at book on display* Is that *Mr Chicken Goes to Paris?*

Me: *smiles* Yes.

International Pashmina: Isn't that funny? Do you know I bought that not long ago at the *Louvre!* *waits for the paroxysms to start*

Me: *smiling* Did you?

International Pashmina: I did! In *Paris!* *waits for my head to explode*

Me: *still smiling*

International Pashmina: How long have you had *Mr Chicken Goes to Paris?*

Me: Ah, about –

International Pashmina: *interrupts* Because I jhust bought it at the LOUVRE! Isn't that FUNNY? *invisible jazz hands*

Me: *still smiling* Mm.

48

Day-off biz bro with a corporate spacemonkey crew cut:
Uhr, hi mate. *drums deal-making brawnmitts on counter*

Me: *smiles* Hullo, mate. How can I help?

Corporate Spacemonkey: I'm looking for a *with his whole mouth* uhwhhhiiine book.

Me: *fascinated* So a wine book?

Corporate Spacemonkey: *blinks; squares shoulders* Yeah.

Me: Sure! We've got the *Halliday Wine Companion* – that's the most popular wine guide – or we've got *lists some others*

Corporate Spacemonkey: *blinks and purses his lips in concentration* Orh. But do you have any, like *strains hard for further words* uhwhine books? Like, just books about uhwhine?

Me: So more of a book about how wine is made, rather than a guide to wines?

Corporate Spacemonkey: *thinks very hard indeed, his eyes taking on the opaque befuddlement of a great white shark's as *it collides with a cage full of divers* Uhr. Just like *makes the shape of a quadrilateral object with his hands* a book more about . . . uhwhine . . . *eyes refocus*

Me: *smiles carefully* Do you mean a book with pictures of wine in it?

Corporate Spacemonkey: *epiphany, like the light of dawn, steals across face; smiles beatifically* Orh. Yeah!

Me: *delighted* We've got heaps.

49

Sunday, 11.45 a.m.

Thirty-something woman with a *Better Homes & Gardens* smile in her voice: Hi. *☺* I'm hoping you can help me.

Me: Hi. *☺* How can I help?

***Better Homes & Gardens* (BHG) Smile:** A friend of mine recommended an older book. *☺* I'm a goose. *☺* I can't remember a title or an author. *☺*

Me: Sure. *☺* What *can* you remember about it? Anything at all. *☺*

BHG Smile: *☺* Oh, good thinking! *☺* It's a classic, she said. I think she said it's about the 1980s, but it was written before then? *☺* Sorry. *☺* That's all I can remember. *☺*

Me: *knows what it is* No, no – that's great – that gives us somewhere to start. *☺* So it's an older book written about . . . the future? *☺*

BHG Smile: Yeah! *☺; twinkles wholesomely* It's a bit of an oldie but a goodie, apparently. *☺*

Me: *enjoys this description enormously* Could it be *1984* by George Orwell?

BHG Smile: *makes the eyes-closed-recognition-of-genius face, like a lifestyle TV host sampling an artisanal beverage* Wow. That's it. *☺* You are wonderful. *☺*

Me: *☺*

50

Wednesday, 3 p.m.

Twinkly mum pushing enormous baby in pram enters store.

Enormous Baby: ROAR!

Me: *jumps*

Twinkly Mum: She just loves bookshops, don't you, Sienna?

Enormous Baby: *strains against pram straps, scrunches up face*

Twinkly Mum: Don't you sweetheart? You love books, don't you?

Enormous Baby: BOOKS!

Me: *jumps*

51

Monday, 12.15 p.m.

Wholesome blonde young mum who turns out to be unspeakably heinous: Hi! *wide-eyed and earnest* Wow! What a beautiful shop. I've never been here before – I mean, I live here, but I've never, like, shopped here before.

Me: *smiles* Thanks – it's a nice shop. How can I help?

Heinous Youngmum: It's wonderful, actually – my amazing sister is having a baby and I want to get her, like, *classic* – CLASSIC – kids' books, 'cause there's just something about books, isn't there? *looks to the heavens, moved by her own eloquence*

Me: *with some weariness* Mmm, there is. So which books did you have in mind? *heading for children's classics* We have some cute Beatrix Potters and some beautifully illustrated classics –

Heinous Youngmum: Yeah – I don't want anything too, like, *old*, you know? I thought it'd be beautiful if I got her the books we loved when *we* were kids, you know? Just to, like, make that link?

Me: *suddenly conscious of stomach contents; swallows* What a great idea! So which books did you guys love?

Heinous Youngmum: Just, like, *claaaasssics* – like the *original* Spot – the one where you look under the tabs – do you have that one?

Me: *scans the pop-up board books* We don't have the small version –

Heinous Youngmum: *wholesome air evaporates; heinous begins* Are you *serious*? *wrinkles nose*

Me: We do have it, but in the larger format –

Heinous Youngmum: *disgusted* I don't want it unless it's the *original*. You seriously don't have it?

Me: I'm sorry – we must have sold out yesterday.

Heinous Youngmum: *sighs theatrically* It's so disappointing to come to an actual, physical bookstore and find you don't have anything I want. *looks at me like I'm a soiled pair of briefs*

Me: *clamps down on sudden rage spike* We'll be getting more in soon – would you like me to order it for you?

Heinous Youngmum: *caustically* Yeah but how long will *that* take?

Me: *sweetly; calmly* I can have one by Thursday.

Heinous Youngmum: *throws up her hands* It seriously takes that long?

Me: It seriously does.

Heinous Youngmum: You're kidding – it takes a *week*?

Me: *looks puzzled* Well, no. Not a week – it's Monday today.

Heinous Youngmum: *turns her back on me and starts to walk away* So you just have nothing . . . God! That's so *disappointing*!

Me: *mood slides Macbethwards* We don't have nothing – there are plenty of other great books here I can recommend. Which other classic kids' books did you and your sister love?

Heinous Youngmum: Do you have Rod Campbell's zoo book? *spitefully* Or do you have to order that one too?

Me: *ignores the spectral dagger shimmering peripherally* Dear Zoo? I'll check for you. *scans section; looks pained* We're out of that one, too – I'm so sorry.

Heinous Youngmum: *shakes head incredulously*

Me: We have Rod Campbell's other zoo book, *My Zoo*.

Heinous Youngmum: *scathingly* But it's not the *original*, is it?

Me: *solemnly* No. No, it is not the original.

Heinous Youngmum: I don't understand how you can stay in business when you don't have anything I want.

Me: *brightly* Funnily enough, it's because we had such a big day yesterday that we don't have the things you want today.

Heinous Youngmum: It's so disappointing to me that you don't have anything.

Me: Well, we run out of things – like you said, we're a physical bookstore, and we have physical limitations. But there's lots here *starts pulling out things* like *Each, Peach, Pear, Plum*, or *The Tiger Who Came to Tea*. Or what about *The Gruffalo*? Or *Where is the Green Sheep*? Or *Animalia*? Or *Puff the Magic Dragon*? Or *Hairy McClary*?

Heinous Youngmum: *disgusted* But these aren't *original* are they?

Me: *strains mightily to think of a way to answer this question that won't seem insulting* . . . No, I suppose they aren't. I'm sorry.

Heinous Youngmum: Wow. Just ridiculous. So you can't help me at all, can you?

Me: *affably* Apparently not.

Heinous Youngmum: This is why people go online. This whole experience has been incredibly disappointing.

Me: Well, all I can say is sorry – if you have any trouble sourcing them online, we'll have them both by the end of the week.

Heinous Youngmum: *dismissively, on her way out* Right.

52

North Shore Bookshop Times **Presents:**

Fun Times Shopping for Men!

A medley of weary female people shopping for the menfolk who diminish their potential and life expectancy by refusing to undertake the necessary rubbing together of the brain sticks to produce the fire that is the thought spark that separates the living organism from, say, the pet rock or the friendly bollard. Let's begin!

Lady being used by her many children as a kind of cat tree: He said he doesn't care what kind of book it is, as long as it's about someone important, like a businessman – but funny.

Me: Does he like Richard Branson?

Lady Cat Tree: No – he thinks he's too educational.

* * *

LADY CAT TREE

Teenage Girl Just Doing Her Best Really (TGJDHBR): He wants a book.

Me: Sure. What kind of book do you think he wants?

TGJDHBR: All he told me was it had to be new because he's read some books this year.

Me: Has he? Well, that's good.

TGJDHBR: He actually doesn't like lots of things, though, so I'm not sure – what new books do you have?

* * *

Older woman who obviously loathes her husband steadily, and with good reason: Can I show this book to my husband? He's just outside – he didn't want to come in.

Me: **bemused** Why didn't he want to come in?

Steady Loather: He says it's too busy.

Me: Are you shopping for a friend?

Steady Loather: **bitterly; keenly; coldly** Oh no – it's for him. He doesn't trust me to pick for him, but he won't come in.

* * *

Heavily pregnant lady with full trolley: Hi! I need a recommendation. My husband wants me to pick up a book for his mother for Christmas.

Me: No worries – did he have anything in mind?

Heavily Pregnant Lady: No – he doesn't know what to get her – he just asked me to choose something she'd like.

Me: Oh. Wow.

53

Harried curly lady: Hi – I'm hoping you can help me – I'm after a book about toilet training, for boys, and it *has* to be *funny*.

Me: Right, we should have something . . . *smiles theatrically* Follow me to one of our most popular sections!

Harried Curly: *browses through several toilet-training titles* This one looks helpful. *narrows eyes and searches cover image of triumphant toddler, chubby fist punching the air, conquered receptacle behind him* But is it *funny*?

Me: *thinks carefully* Well, maybe not that funny . . . What about *Pirate Potty*?

Harried Curly: No, he's frightened of pirates.

Me: *nods sagely* Fair enough. I think that's probably our funniest toilet-training book, though. Maybe take the helpful one and see how he goes?

Harried Curly: *unequivocally, with a chopping motion of the hand for emphasis* No! It HAS to be FUNNY! He won't do ANYTHING unless it's funny!

54

Sunday, 10.40 a.m.

Middle-aged man with an outpatient haircut, in shorts and a puffer jacket, carrying an apple in one hand and a carrot in the other, enters store with a sullen, slightly furtive air and heads straight for the back corner, home of the architecture books – a shoplifter's delight.

Me: *smiles blandly and says good morning; launches full Terminator scan in base of covert operations behind smiling, bespectacled eyes* [Initial results suggest reclusive, single male with libertarian and/or spiritual 'practitioner' tendencies. Single item of fruit; single item of vegetable suggests gut neurosis: possible clean eater/yoga smug/tantric sex workshop/erectile dysfunction. Puffer jacket: possible past as currency trader/ IT professional. Divorced. HAIRCUT? Inconclusive. Risk of theft: low. Suggested action: monitor casually in overhead anti-theft mirror, with option to engage SmileHelp tactical strike should need arise.]

Outpatient Haircut: *sits on chair in architecture section; pulls up large, expensive book full of buildings and starts in on apple*

Me: *glances at overhead mirror from time to time; vaguely annoyed by a grown man in shorts and a puffer jacket eating an apple over an expensive book like a pre-schooler at snack time; not entirely sure he isn't an incredibly amateurish thief*

Outpatient Haircut: *finishes apple; puts core down; starts in on carrot*

Me: *stares at overhead mirror* [POSSIBLE CONTAMINATION: ARCHITECTURE SECTION. Locating unaccounted food waste . . .]

Outpatient Haircut: *catches me looking in mirror; glares, half-surly, half-sulky, at my distorted reflection; bites savagely into carrot*

Me: [FOOD WASTE LOCATED. CONTAMINATION. BREACH BREACH BREACH. DEPLOY] *swoops across store; looms over Outpatient Haircut like a storm front, brow ridges at maximum overhang*

Outpatient Haircut: Oh, will you just leave me alone! You've been watching me since I came in! I suppose you're going to ask to look in my bag! *glares*

Me: *narrows eyes hawkishly* No, not at all. *Eastwood pause; menacingly and with teeth* I'm going to ask you to take that wet apple core you had your mouth on a moment ago off the display shelf – it's almost touching a very expensive book, and it's disgusting.

Outpatient Haircut: *shrinks into his appalling haircut* Oh. Sorry. *puts apple core in puffer jacket pocket*

Me: *Disappears silently between the shelves, plaid shirt flapping like a cape*

55

Perpetually frowning woman in camel coat with many jewels:
Hello, I'm in a rush and my mother has turned 100.

Me: *buffering* . . . Wow. How can I help?

Frowncamel: I just want something small for her birthday,
something appropriate for someone who's just turned 100
– do you have anything like that?

Me: Do I have a small gift appropriate for your mother who
has just turned 100?

Frowncamel: *grows frownier* Yes.

Me: *fascinated* I have no idea! What sort of small gift *is* appropriate for a 100-year-old lady? What sort of 100-year-old
lady is your mother? *starry-eyed; drifting* Wow! Imagine
– 100 years old . . .

Frowncamel: *impatiently* Just something small – I'm in a
rush – something like a notebook.

Me: *deflates* I'll show you where they are.

FROWNCAMEL

56

Rough, Oakley-wearing, tortoise-necked man with sunburn, a thick gold chain, and a singlet that reads, 'DO NOT DISTURB – Already Disturbed': Mate, what murder books have you got?

57

Tuesday, 2.30 p.m.

Demonic child with bowl cut runs into shop, trailed slowly and vaguely by wafting mother. Manager and I exchange poisonous looks.

Manager: It's not a good place for running, sweetheart!

Bowl Cut Demon Child: *giggles impudently; keeps running between the shelves*

Waftmum: *like a gentle breeze* Will, slow down now, sweetie ... *stops to look at display table*

Me and Manager: *side eyes*

Manager: *to Waftmum, with heroic diplomacy* If he trips he might hurt himself – there are a lot of sharp edges in here –

Bowl Cut Demon Child, still giggling maniacally, makes full lap of shop, takes the corner into the children's section too fast, trips over his own feet, hurtles through the air, hits his head on the side of a plywood shelf with a loud thud, and faceplants spectacularly into the carpet.

Manager: *phlegmatically* That's why it's not a good place for running.

Me: *turns away to hide deep satisfaction*

58

Saturday, 11 a.m.

Incredibly hostile woman (IHW): *aggressively* I need a gift voucher!

Me: *blinks* Okay. I can do you one of those.

IHW: *through clenched teeth* Good.

Me: How much?

IHW: WHAT?

Me: *calmly* How much would you like the voucher to be worth?

IHW: *angrily* Oh, I don't know! How much should it be?

Me: *deeply fascinated by this* Well, it can be any value you want – how much would you like it to be?

IHW: I DON'T KNOW! What's a book worth?

Me: *starting to enjoy himself* Well, it depends on the book.

IHW: *really, really annoyed* Well what's a NORMAL one worth?

Me: *bemused* A normal one? Depends . . .

IHW: Oh, for Christ's sake! Is it something like $25 or something?

Me: *blinks benignly* $25? Sure! *taps keyboard with a flourish* That's $25. *smiles*

IHW: *seethes; pays*

59

Sunday, 3.35 p.m.

Heroically old lady with walking cane calls out from the far corner of the counter: Excuse me!

Me: *finishes up with a customer; hurries over* How can I help?

Heroically Old Lady: *holds up a card* Is this card blank?

Me: *smiles encouragingly* It is.

Heroically Old Lady: *peers at it* How do I get words inside it?

Me: *staggers mentally; recovers* Would you like to write in it?

Heroically Old Lady: How can I congratulate my friend if there aren't any words inside it?

Me: You could write her a message.

Heroically Old Lady: *ruminates on this* I think I better come around there – *gathers up card, cane, and handbag; proceeds to front of the counter* Can you show me how to open it?

Me: Of course. *opens up the card* So you can write your friend a message here. *points out blank section of card*

Heroically Old Lady: Oh. I see. So I'd write in there?

Me: *nods companionably*

Heroically Old Lady: Right. *pays for the card; pulls a wrapped present out of her purse; thinks carefully* I think I need a pen.

Me: I've got one.

Heroically Old Lady: *takes the pen; carefully writes 'Dear C—, Congratulations on your birthday. With best wishes, M—', then hands the card back*

Me: *takes the card, fits it into the envelope, tucks the envelope under the ribbon of present* There we go.

Heroically Old Lady: Thank you, young man. *surveys her work proudly then looks bemused* I'm very old.

Me: *thinks very carefully* You've got beautiful handwriting.

60
Sunday, 2.45 p.m.

Recipe: Le Turducken de Poseur

Close-cropped middle-aged man, Italian styling, designer frames, puts down soft black leather case embossed 'DEUS', places unopened pack of Moleskine notebooks beside case, takes a half-step back, rests finger against lip, and ponders.

Close-Crop: Hmmm . . .

Me: . . . Hmmm?

Close-Crop: Hmmm, maybe you can help. Do you think these notebooks will fit in my beautiful case? *opens case to reveal iPad mini and assorted fancy pens* I want to just slip one under my iPad.

Me: *lavishly* Shall we open the pack and find out?

Close-Crop: *titillated* Ooh! Could we?

Me: *Nigellaishly* Let's dare greatly. *opens pack, slips a notebook under the iPad*

Close-Crop: It fits perfectly. *closes case with a small, contented sigh* It's complete.

61

Monday, 5.20 p.m.

Older woman with a remarkable amount of food on her face: Do you have a photocopier on the premises?

Me: *cagily* Why?

Old Foodface: I need some copying done. I'll pay you.

Me: No, we don't do copying, I'm afraid – you could try the newsagent?

Old Foodface: *produces a sheaf of handwritten pages; maddens visibly* It's very urgent. I need to Express Post it in the next twenty minutes.

Me: What is it?

Old Foodface: It's a letter to Scott Morrison about the Chinese.

62

Sunday, 1.30 p.m.

Beachbound dudebro and his dead letter bureau (DLB) girl-friend trundle through the store with their beach biz until they reach the back of the shop where I'm receiving stock at the back counter in a kind of fugue state.

Beachbound Dudebro: *stumbles on the graphic novels* Aw, sick! Hay, Michelle! I found my section, hay. Fucken *Tintin* was tha best, hay?

DLB: *blank silence*

Beachbound Dudebro: If you ever wanna buy me anything, buy me fucken *Tintin* – I wanna get all of them, hay.

DLB: *test pattern*

Beachbound Dudebro: *casts about for someone to witness his transport; glimpses me behind a pile of books* Dude, this shop is sick!

Me: *smiles dimly; goes back to receiving stock*

BEACHBOUND
DUDEBRO AND
DEAD LETTER
BUREAU
GIRLFRIEND

Beachbound Dudebro: *to everyone; to the air; to history* It's funny how they call it graphic novels, hay? It's like – NAH! they're all just CARTOONS!

Me: ... *receiving*

Beachbound Dudebro: Funny, hay?

Me: *dimly realises a response is expected; answers from within the fugue* ... It's like how novels used to be called wordbooks.

Beachbound Dudebro: *makes a face like a man on a speeding motorbike doing algebra* Really?

Me: *snorts awake mentally; blinks; concedes* No, not really.

Beachbound Dudebro: ...

Me: ...

Beachbound Dudebro: ... AAAWWWWhahahahaha! *nudges DLB* This c-nt! *points at this c-nt*

DLB: *guffaws*

Me: *preens like Oscar Wilde*

63

Thursday, 5 p.m.

Tortoiseshell Woman: I just had to buy this – it's adorable!

hands over birthday card with Eiffel Tower on it

Me: *blearily* Mmm. Great card, great card . . .

Tortoiseshell Woman: I love Paris. I just love it!

Me: *obsequiously* What is it that you particularly love about it?

Tortoiseshell: . . .

Me: . . .

Tortoiseshell: . . .

Me: . . .

Tortoiseshell: . . .

Me: $6.50.

64

Kempt older lady with a strangulated voice and a tendency towards unsettling amounts of eye contact: Hello. I'm looking for the latest book by Charles Krauthammer. I'm not quite sure what it's called.

Me: *smiles pleasantly because he doesn't know who Charles Krauthammer is* Let me check for you. *Googles; blanches invisibly* His latest book is *Things That Matter* – we don't have it, I'm afraid.

Kempt Strangulator: Oh. Will you be getting it?

Me: *truthfully; concealing relief* Unfortunately, it's out of print with the Australian distributor.

Kempt Strangulator: What if I came back in, say, a month?

Me: *untruthfully* It's possible. *smiles blandly*

Kempt Strangulator: Can you check another title by Juan Williams?

Me: Sure – what's the title?

Kempt Strangulator: *Muzzled.* It's about free speech and political correctness.

Me: *smiles; smoothes over anything that might be taken as interest or intelligence or opinion in his expression* I'll check . . . *truthfully; relieved* Same again, I'm afraid. Sorry about that! *drops polite portcullis on conversation: steps back, half-crosses arms, looks over Kempt Strangulator's shoulder*

Kempt Strangulator: *finds it impossible not to explain* They're both very interesting writers – just really clear, crisp, *logical* writers. *hunts my eyes, which are now floating limply behind my glasses like captive dolphins* Williams is really passionate about free speech – they both just really *cut *gestures violently* through.

Me: *gives absolutely no response*

Kempt Strangulator: *attempts at eye contact become more violent; head moves from side to side in a snake-like, distance-judging motion* Krauthammer's a really *logical* guy – *pauses; looks rueful* though he doesn't think Trump would make a good president. *eye lasers resume* What do you think?

Me: *with Labrador blandness* I suppose we'll have to find out more about what he actually thinks to know.

Kempt Strangulator: *lights up but visibly restrains herself; muscles in neck squirm* I think you need to be careful about that. Trump's actually written quite a lot if you look – but I think the media has something against him – so you need to be careful. *hoods eyes*

Me: *smilingly; noddingly; rhetorically* Really? Right. *nods some more*

Kempt Strangulator: Yes, you need to be very careful at the moment. I think political correctness has really just run wild – and – you know, I'll probably offend you saying this – but the media is – it just approaches everything from a – the way they report things and how they *slant* things – it's just so *cups a hand over the side of her face, as if they (who? Robespierre?) are listening* Left, you know?

Me: *pleasantly; temperately; slowly* Hmm. It's funny, isn't it? I suspect I'm on the other end of the political spectrum to you – I approach things from the Left and think of myself as a Leftist – and me and a lot of my friends also think the media focuses on the wrong things.

Kempt Strangulator: *more neck squirming* Hmm. *fatuously* It's about values, really, isn't it?

Me: *smiles like a pool toy*

Kempt Strangulator: Well, I'll come back in a month to look for those books – thank you for your honest opinion. Goodbye!

Me: Have a good day! *turns; reflexively sanitizes hands*

65

Elderly gentleman with a tie on under his jumper, peering drolly over a very fine pair of tortoise-shell spectacles: *in a quiet, confiding English drawl* I hear you've a new le Carré . . .

Me: *delighted* We do indeed! Let me just check to see if it's still in stock.

Very Fine Tortoise: *makes a harummm face* I suppose they're selling like *gathers himself* Hhot Cakes.

Me: *conceals his joy with great effort*

66

Saturday, 9 a.m.

First customer of the day, long-faced European woman, trailing busy-handed children who wreck two displays on the way through the door to the counter.

Euro Longface: Hi, I need suhm helpe. *weary sigh* I need a suggestion for a ten-year-old ghirl. *ignores children madly scrabbling to touch every book on the counter*

Me: *feeling very sad and tired of work already* Sure! What kind of girl is she? Does she like to read?

Euro Longface: We dhon't know her fvery well, *more sighing* bhut she has been in hospital a lhot lately . . . *trails off as if this should prompt me*

Me: *wishing for an earthquake or a stampede of bison* Oh, that's no good. *frowns sympathetically* So what kind of thing do you think would help? Would you like something to help cheer her up?

Euro Longface: *from a long way away mentally* I dhon't know – she has had cancer so perhaps she does not whant to be cheered up – perhaps a book about a brave girl that is not too happy. Do you have something like this?

Me: Oh . . . Well . . . Let me see what I can think of . . . *sinks into despond*

67

Wednesday, 1.15 p.m.

Flustered blonde lady in a hectic flush rush: Hi! I was just here!

Me: I remember – how can I help?

Hectic Flushrush: You gave me the wrong book. *pulls out the copy of* Harry Potter and the Cursed Child *she bought 20 minutes earlier* This is the play!

Me: Oh no!

Hectic Flushrush: I drove straight back once I realised! So can I swap this for the actual book?

Me: *looks pained* I'm so sorry – this is the actual book –

Hectic Flushrush: No! *Really?*

Me: *clasps hands together* Really. It's the script of the play being performed in the UK.

Hectic Flushrush: *stricken* BUT WHY WOULD SHE *DO* THAT?

Me: *shakes head and smiles ruefully* I don't know. I'm sorry. Do you want to swap it for something else?

Hectic Flushrush: *looks utterly miserable* No, no – if this is it, then this is it – I have to read it! But it's SO SAD! I'm SO DISAPPOINTED!

Me: I'm sorry. Me too.

Hectic Flushrush: *desperately* Do you know if it's any good?

Me: *shamefacedly* I'm . . . not sure. Maybe it's great; maybe it's . . . *shrugs*

Hectic Flushrush: *still stricken* It's a PLAY?!

Me: *chuckles* Exactly.

68

Sunday, 3.25 p.m.

Pantomime hoodlum, complete with Polo Ralph Lauren hat, manscaped eyebrows, stained varsity grey jumper, and scuffed-up white slip-ons prowls into the store, scoping out the mirrors and corners until his eyes meet mine.

Me: *smilingly, from behind the counter where I've been watching him since he came in* Hello, mate!

Pantomime Hood: *makes an exasperated noise, throws his hands in the air, and walks out*

Me: *laughs helplessly*

Everything takes practice; we all start somewhere.

PANTOMIME HOOD

69

Saturday, 9.30 a.m.

Me: *answers phone*

Gladys on the Phone: Hello? This is Gladys.

Me: Hello Gladys! How can I help?

Gladys on the Phone: I have a friend who isn't well in hospital and she can't really read anything so I want to get her just a little funny thing about cats – do you have something?

Me: *affably* We should do – we have a lot of little funny things about cats.

Gladys on the Phone: What've you got? Have you got something just small on the counter, something like 'what my cat taught me' or 'life according to a cat' – something little like that?

Me: So we've got *Cats in Sweaters* – that's cute pictures of cats in knitted jumpers –

Gladys on the Phone: *perturbed* Oh yes?

Me: And *Artists and Their Cats* – that's a collection of photo portraits of famous artists and their cats – it's got Salvador Dali and a *very* attractive cat on the cover –

Gladys on the Phone: *appalled* Oh.

Me: We've also got *If It Fits I Sits: Cats in Awkward Places* – that's mainly pictures of cats in Tupperware –

Gladys on the Phone: *horrified* Oh!

Me: We've also got *The Beauty of Cats* and *Cats on Instagram* – a collection of the finest cats on the internet. Do any of those seem right? *maniacally* We've got more!

Gladys on the Phone: *clearly worried* Oh. I'm not sure now. I'll have to look further into it. Are you open tomorrow?

Me: Ten to four.

Gladys on the Phone: I'd better come in then and have a look . . .

Me: See you tomorrow, Gladys!

Gladys on the Phone: *primly* Yes. *hangs up*

70

Small, fierce mustelid lady with an aggressive credit card hand: Just that! *darts book on to counter* And I need to pay with this! *stabs credit card at machine* But I'm not sure what's left on it or how much I've spent!

Me: No problem – let's see how we go. *scans book* That's $29.99.

Mustelady: *stabs machine with card*

Me: *breezily* Yep, that's gone through.

Mustelady: *giggles ferociously; shows teeth*

Me: *smiles to hide his terror* You're rich!

Mustelady: *fiercely* I *am* rich.

Me: *heartily* Good for you!

Mustelady: *with a red light in her eyes* This is just my SPENDING money – I am ... I have a lot MORE.

Me: *keeps his movements slow and small* Well, then, the sky's the limit – you can go on a spree.

Mustelady: I CAN! *picks up book* This is just the start. I'm going to COLES next! *darts out of store in direction of Coles*

71

Friday, 3 p.m.

Jacketed Gen X insinuator of the Charles Waterstreet genus:
He-ey *drums fingers on counter needlessly*

Me: *douses this flagrant bit of posturing in the tranquil sea of service sector courtesy* Hello! How can I help?

Jacketed Insinuator: *clearly annoyed at having his cool approach thwarted* Do you guys have a copy of the *2016 Drug Handbook*? I looked but I *runs a ringed hand through his greying locks* couldn't find it.

Me: *checking* No, sorry . . . We had it but we've sold out. We don't usually get many in – would you like me to order one for you?

Jacketed Insinuator: Wow.

Me: *twinkles* Wow. Sorry. Shall I get one in?

Jacketed Insinuator: *with no encouragement whatsoever* When I was at uni, every share house had one. So we knew what we could dose.

Me: *smiles blandly* Is that right?

Jacketed Insinuator: *shakes out his locks again* Yeah, I mean what do you guys even *do* at uni these days?

Me: *blinks demurely* Work, mostly.

Jacketed Insinuator: *snorts* Well that's *boring.*

Me: *twinkles again* It is. Would you like me to order you one in?

72

Saturday, 10 a.m.

Low-fringed, sandblasted blonde woman with the pugnacious, snap-hinge mouth of a monitor lizard: I want Jane Harper's *The Dry*!

Me: *feels the residual calm equipoise of his recent holiday leave him in a rush of sadness and irritation* Good morning! I'll get you one – won't be a sec. *heads for the crime section*

Sandblasted Snap-Mouth: *follows testily* You probably don't have any left – I couldn't see it! *snaps mouth shut*

Me: *twinkles* Here it is! *hands it over*

Sandblasted Snap-Mouth: *annoyed* Where was it?!

Me: *winces at the redundancy* It was here *pats shelf* in the crime section, under H, where it's supposed be for a change. *smiles confidingly*

Sandblasted Snap-Mouth: *even more annoyed* Yeah but why was it HERE?

Me: *baffled* In the crime section?

SANDBLASTED
SNAP-MOUTH

Sandblasted Snap-Mouth: *enraged* Yeah! *snaps mouth shut*

Me: *ponders this* . . . Because it's a crime novel?

Sandblasted Snap-Mouth: *furious* NO! Why isn't it more obvious!? It's a BEST SELLER!

Me: Oh. *digests this* Ah . . . *snaps mouth shut* Hmmm . . . *retreats; feels the extent to which he is now back at work*

73

Wry lady of the kind and vintage that licks her fingers before she touches money: Fred Vargas – is this all you've got by her? *nods at* The Accordionist *on the counter*

Me: Not sure – let me check for you. *checks computer* Yeah, that's it, I'm afraid. It's the new one.

Wrylick: *pulls a wry face* Oh well, I better have it. *licks her fingers and pulls two twenties* It's funny, I had a whole heap of her books and couldn't come at them at first – now I love them.

Me: *smiles pleasantly while he takes the lickmoney* Yeah, it's funny like that sometimes –

Wrylick: And I found out she was a woman, which was *very* interesting. Why would you call yourself Fred?

Me: *pompously* For the money, probably – and so her work didn't get pigeonholed. *warms to his subject* There's a long history of women writers publishing under male pseudonyms so their work would be taken seriously – like George Eliot, the Brontës –

Wrylick: *cuts me off* Yes, yes, yes, I know all that! But why *Fred*?

Me: Ah, right, I see ... *stumped* ... Yeah wow ... Good question.

74

Trendy mum in stripes, slip-ons, and three-quarter jeans, accompanied by small daughter: We'll take this one. *hands over kid's activity book with high rainbow content*

Me: *smiles* Great! Looks like fun.

Trendy Mum: *earnestly* I have to tell you – and you probably get this all the time – you have a really beautiful face. I was just looking at you from over there, and the shape *draws imaginary lines with thumb and forefinger over own face* – your face is beautiful. *laughs* Is that alright to say? It probably sounds weird. *laughs*

Me: *giggles; flaps hand* No, no – thank you – that's very kind – I'll hold on to that one, it's a lovely compliment, and I definitely don't get it all the time.

Trendy Mum: I just had to tell you –

Me: No, no, thanks again –

Trendy Mum: *nods earnestly* Just a really beautiful face . . .

Me: *blushes outrageously*

75

Sunday, 11.15 a.m.

Dead-eyed haircut with the little Ralph Lauren horse golf player perched over his knitwear nipple: Hello – do you have any of Andrew Bolt's works?

Me: *assumes the Snorlax smile of hapless obstructionism* I'll check – I think we've sold out of his latest – we've had problems with the supplier.

Horse Nipple Haircut: It's not for me, obviously – my father wants it for Father's Day.

Me: *still Snorlaxing* Yeah, sorry, doesn't look like we have it.

Horse Nipple Haircut: *with absolutely no encouragement* Though I did see him speak at the Festival of Dangerous Ideas – it was actually fascinating. *muses sagely* It seemed very important.

Me: Ah, the Festival of Dangerous Ideas – what a varied program of speakers they must have! *twinkles vacuously*

Horse Nipple Haircut: Yes, it's an excellent festival. I'll just get him this, then. *drops John Cleese's latest musings from *tax exile on counter; hazards a joke** Not that they have anything to do with each other.

Me: *feels the phrase 'Well, it's funny you should say that' forming like a cloud bank; ruthlessly disperses it** John Cleese is a very funny man. $24.99.

76

Really delightful lady, after having a long and funny chat with me about her son's fantasy reading, notices *Nutshell* (the novel in which Ian McEwan imbues a foetus with the personality and politics of *The Australian* opinions page) on the counter: Is that Ian McEwan's new one?

Me: It is – are you a fan?

Really Delightful Lady: I am a *big* fan, but isn't this the one about the foetus?

Me: Yeah, probably not his best idea ever. Once you get famous enough, though, people will put up with a lot.

Really Delightful Lady: *thoughtfully* You should probably warn people about it.

Me: In the sense that it might offend people?

Really Delightful Lady: Well – personifying foetuses – it's pretty sensitive.

Me: Do you mean religiously?

Really Delightful Lady: No, no, in terms of foetal rights and things like that. For women who've had an abortion – I've had an abortion – it's pretty uncomfortable. And then there's Zoe's Law and all that stuff. Personifying a foetus is a big part of granting it rights.

Me: *thoroughly embarrassed* Christ. I hadn't even thought about that.

Really Delightful Lady: *smiles much more kindly than she should* Well, that's the thing, isn't it?

Me: *ruefully* That's exactly the thing.

77

Burlyposh Northern Englishman bristling with restrained rage: *pulls a copy of Hillary Clinton's* What Happened *and cheesy Christmas card with the Sydney Harbour Bridge on it out of a brown paper bag* There's been a Christmas dooble-oop on the book and the card as well – I was given these as a gift and I've already got them – I wan'a refoond *menaces the EFTPOS machine with a quick-drawn credit card*

Me: *gingerly; caught on the back foot* Oh, I'm sorry to hear that – even the card! Sadly, we don't –

Burlyposh: *cuts me off; puts his finger in my face* Don't tell me I can't have a refund! I worked in Australian retail for five years and I know I'm entitled to one by law – I'll have it on my card, please!

Me: *staggered by unexpected rage spike triggered by finger in the face; brain pumping pure sriracha sauce; jaw and hands clench* I'm sorry – we don't do refunds – I can do you an exchange or a voucher –

Burlyposh: *cuts me off again* Well I was told when I bought it I could have one! And I never shop anywhere that doosn't accept re-TURNS! *gets further into my face, vein bulging in his forehead*

Me: *breaks eye contact and checks Burlyposh's receipt as a way of calming down; consciously slows breathing* I'm sorry, I can do you an exchange or an exchange voucher –

Burlyposh: No, that's no good to me! I'm goin' back overseas soon – I'm not from here – I want a *leans into it* re-foond and I'm entitled to it by law! I've been in Australian retail for *holds up four fingers* FOUR YEARS and I've dealt with this sort of thing a thousand times – I know exactly how to take it further if I need to. *breathes out; seethes* I know it's the LAW!

Me: *notes the discrepancy between five and four years in 'Australian retail'; likewise notes that the book and card were impossibly both purchased by Burlyposh and received as a gift; understands Burlyposh is blagging; takes hold of temper; reverts to calm* I can offer you an exchange or a voucher. We don't refund.

Burlyposh: *leans in again* You *have* to – by *law* –

Me: *also leans in, with a bland, conciliatory smile, like a pool toy on the attack* We only have to offer a refund if the product is faulty or unfit for purpose – so if the book had pages missing, or if I'd sold it to you as a biography of Trump rather than Hillary Clinton, then you'd have grounds – as it is I can give you an exchange voucher or you can swap it for something else.

Burlyposh: *steps back; reddens further* Where is your policy written?!

Me: *takes up Burlyposh's receipt* It's written on the bottom of your receipt – *reads it in a calm, even voice*

Burlyposh: *snarls* That's RIDICULOUS! I know *stabs finger* my *rights* *stabs finger* by *law!* *extra long stab*

Me: *waits*

Burlyposh: *tries a glare*

Me: *goes blank; waits*

Burlyposh: *incredulously* So you're not giving me a refoond?
Me: *neutral expression* No.

Burlyposh: *grasping now* Well. That's very bad Christmas service, then, isn't it?

Me: *earnestly* I'm sorry to hear that. Would you like the exchange voucher, or do you want to pick something else?

Burlyposh: *dwindling into wounded self-righteousness, like Thornton facing the workers* Is that all you can give me?

Me: It is.

Burlyposh: *makes a disgusted gesture that means 'proceed'* I'll be taking this further – I know exactly how to do it!

Me: *processes the voucher, shows Burlyposh where to sign* I understand. There's your voucher, and make sure you hold on to that receipt – that's the record of this transaction with my signature at the bottom.

Burlyposh: I've doon it a thousand times, mate – it's going to be easy.

Me: *nods and smiles* All the best with it.

Burlyposh: *stalks out holding his voucher*

Me: *smiles him out the door and round the corner; sags; breathes out through clenched teeth; punches the counter; arranges his face; smiles at the queue* Who was next?

78

Solemn ten year old in blue velour hoodie: *shyly* Hello.

Me: *twinkling* Hello. Do you need some help?

Solemnten: Can you tell me – *thinks seriously for a moment* – can you tell me what exactly the new Harry Potter book *is*?

Me: *ruefully* It's a play – it's a written-down version of the stage play they're showing in London at the moment.

Solemnten: *lowers brows* It's a *script*?

Me: *makes sympathetic face* It's a script.

Solemnten: *stricken* Why?

Me: Good question, kid. Good question.

79
Monday, 5.25 p.m.

Woman in black-and-white-striped top and dark cardigan slides winged shades up her long, patrician nose to her forehead, deftly pinning back her coal-grey bangs: *with cool world-weariness* Hi, are you still open? Do you have Patti Smith's *M Train*?

Me: *delighted* Yes! *gathers himself; does his best to effect a lazy Lou Reed nonchalance* Ah-um, I mean, yeah. *hoods his eyes; puts his hands in his pockets* Yeah, we do.

80

Saturday, 12.30 p.m.

Me: *seated at wrapping table working through a huge pile of Father's Day tat*

Beach-blonde lady with a brain runnier than a lightly poached egg, from over my shoulder: What are yeeeeew deeewwwing?

Me: *cringes invisibly; half-turns* I'm wrapping presents.

Beach-poached: Aaaeww! You're doing a wonderful job!

Me: *thinly* Thanks. *continues doing a wonderful job*

Beach-poached: It makes me want to have something wrapped!

Me: *wanly* Mm. Well, you're welcome to have something wrapped – it's free.

Beach-poached: Aaaeww! Wow! How do I do it? Do I just ask you?

Me: *tying a ribbon* You do. But first you'll need to buy something.

Beach-poached: But what should I buy?!

Me: *wrapping with increasing speed* Well, we're a bookshop – you could buy a book?

Beach-poached: What a good idea! I haven't bought a book in such a long time! *thinks performatively* What should I buy?

Me: *cheerfully; with hate deep in his wrapping heart* Why don't you go and have a browse to get some ideas, and then come back when you're ready?

Beach-poached: I will! What fun! *wanders into the shop*

Me: *finishes wrapping, goes on lunchbreak, rests head in hands*

81

Saturday, 10.05 a.m.

Very old, very weird chameleon lady, dressed entirely in blue, zeroes in on me behind the counter and begins to speak very quickly.

Old Weird Chameleon Lady (OWCL): I want a book for a mother and a baby all about mothers and babies and what they do together in life. *focuses on my face with one eye and then the other*

Me: *blinks; downloads information* So you want a book about a mother having a child, for children?

OWCL: Yes, something about what they do and how that operates in a day-to-day sense but for a baby. *eyes seem to move independently of each other*

Me: *straining very hard* So a book about mothers and babies for a baby about what mothers and babies do . . . *this linguistic Escher sketch fails to clarify anything for anyone*

OWCL: *focuses with one eye, then the other*

Me: *starts to sweat; lunges desperately at a thought* Do you mean a book for a child about their mother having a baby? About having a baby brother or sister?

OWCL: *both eyes narrow* No, I mean a book for a baby about what its mother does with it such as going to the park and in the stroller, and about how its mother cares for it – do you have a book about that?

Me: *losing cabin pressure* . . . Around the world? *re-calibrates mentally* As in, what mothers do with babies around the world?

OWCL: No, a normal mother and baby in a normal day in the stroller going to the park smiling at each other.

Me: *mental gravity fails* Wow. So a kind of day in the life of a baby and a mother for a baby. *bemused* Like James Joyce for babies.

OWCL: *one eye; then the other*

Me: *drifting into space* I don't think we have a book like that . . .

OWCL: Oh that's alright I didn't think you would.

82

Sunday, 12.10 p.m.

Quietly and happily receiving some stock in the back office when the front counter bell rings – walk out to find my colleague Steph ready to tag out after a few rounds with a taut, nervous woman with the mad, rolling eyes of that horse that jumps off the boat in the English version of the Japanese horror film *The Ring*.

Steph: *in her usual polite, factual way* I told her she could exchange or get a credit, but she couldn't have a refund. She wants a refund. *clears the area*

Me: Right. *faces up to Taut Ringhorse* So how can I help?

Taut Ringhorse: *in a strangled, angry rush* My husband bought these yesterday *gestures at three baby books with a combined value of less than $30* and the woman he spoke to said he could have a refund if they weren't right and you have to give me one because these books are unfit for purpose and the people we wanted to give them to already have them and it's a disaster! *eyes roll, neck muscles squirm convulsively*

Me: *calmly and kindly* I sold these to your husband yesterday *recalls a slack-jawed weekend business idiot in a grey T-shirt* and I told him we don't do refunds. But we can swap them for something else or I can give you an exchange voucher –

Taut Ringhorse: *with tears in her voice* But they're unfit for purpose! I'm entitled to a refund!

Me: *sighs* You're only entitled to a refund if the product is faulty or was sold to you under –

Taut Ringhorse: *wells up, gulps a breath*

Me: *sighs again* – but I'll refund you this time and you'll know next time.

Taut Ringhorse: *sniffs* Oh thank you! Thank you so much!

Me: *smiles wearily* That's alright.

Taut Ringhorse: *fervently* You're so *kind.* *gulps again* Thank you!

Me: *queasily* That's alright. I hope your day improves.

Taut Ringhorse: Oh, it will! Thank you! *smiles through watery eyes*

83

Vectors

Tired mum with very red, raw nostrils hands over *Thomas the Tank Engine* book while her small son snivels and watches on.

Me: *foolishly picks up* Thomas *book to scan it*￼ You guys look like you've had a rough week.

Tired Nostrils: *gummily* Yeah, we've both been sick – he's been miserable! We had to come out today – we were going crazy at home! *sucks back something chicken-soupish through her soft palate*

Small Snivels: *lets go of his mother's leg, reaches for the front of the counter, opens his mouth and mumbles the wood with his teeth*

Me: *watches Small Snivels gum the counter, transfixed*

* * *

Apologetic British mum with boy who looks very close to death sitting in her trolley hands over a picture book: Hi. Sorry about the trolley – he's very unwell and I'm trying to cheer him up.

Me: That's alright! *foolishly moves closer to the pestilential child to scan the book* There's a horrible cold going around this year, which is weird considering how hot it's been.

BritMum: *apologetically* He's had scarlet fever – I've just taken him to the doctor for some antibiotics.

Me: Wow! Scarlet fever! That's very *Jane Eyre. *bags the dying child's book*

BritMum: Yes, the doctor said it's making a comeback.

Me: *smiles companionably* Thanks for bringing him in.

BritMum: *apologetically* Oh, he's just had some antibiotics so he's probably not contagious anymore.

84
Tuesday, 9.30 a.m.

Crazed lady in yoga pants: Oh! *gasps hectically* I've just always loved books! *writhes*

Me: . . .

Crazed Pants: Oh! *eyes bulge*

Me: *relents* Mm, they're pretty good, aren't they?

Crazed Pants: They. Are. Wonderful!

Me: Was there a particular book you were looking for?

Crazed Pants: Oh! Not today – I've just had a class.

Me: . . .

Crazed Pants: I wanted to come in and see them!

CRAZED PANTS

85

Sunday, 10.30 a.m.

Me: *answers the phone*

Kathy, whose TV is very loud at 10.30 am, even over the phone: *shouting over the TV* Hi, it's Kathy T— hee-yer!

Me: Hi Kathy! How can I help?

Kathy TV: *in the scorched, word-snapping accents of deepest, darkest Brookvale* I think I got a message from yow – I think m'book's c'm in!

Me: No worries, Kathy, let me check – what's the book?

Kathy TV: *shouting over the TV* It's the Jackie Collins!

Me: *now also shouting over the TV* Right – do you know which one?

Kathy TV: Yep. The last one of [long-running series involving sexy mobsters, sexy money, sexy houses, and sexy sex]!

Me: *cheerfully; still shouting* Yep – we've got it here for you, Kathy!

Kathy TV: Good! *tsks as she thinks; continues to shout* I don't know if I c'n come up this afternoon! *aggressively, as if she suspects I'll refuse* Will you hold on to it for me till next Fri-dey?

Me: *one finger in other ear* No worries, Kathy! Take your time! We hold for two weeks so there's no rush!

Kathy TV: *made suspicious by my easy tone* Y'won't get rid of it, will yow?

Me: *unavoidable mental image of Kathy as cockatoo with her head cocked to one side, peering into the phone with a dubious, scaly eye* No, definitely not! It'll be here for you when you come in!

Kathy TV: *suddenly sunny again* Ow, good! *confidingly* I love these books! They're exciting, they've got crime and sexy stuff in 'em! Rubbish, but I luv'm!

Me: *bellowing* They sound great! And you need some rubbish – it's an important part of a balanced reading diet!

Kathy TV: *slyly; loudly* Ow, so you like books with sexy stuff in 'em too, do yow?

Me: *Dr Hibbert giggle* Kathy, I have to go now – you have a good day!

Kathy TV: *cackles* Good on ya, mate, good on ya! I'll be in next Fri-dey!

86

Saturday, 11.25 a.m.

Older English lady wearing thick eyeliner and a very sensible straw sun hat, like Angela Carter on a beach holiday: *briskly* Yes, good morning, do you have the new Jamie Oliver, please?

Me: We do! *fetches it* I hear it's very good.

Beach Carter: Yes, it's not for me, it's for my husband. *looks drily amused* After forty years of marriage, he's suddenly become interested in cooking – the shit!

Me: *slain*

87

Saturday, 9.15 a.m.

Deceptively kind-faced woman: Hi – I'm hoping your manager is here . . .

Me: No, sorry, not today – was there something in particular you needed help with?

Deceptive Kind-Face: I actually need a really good recom-mendation, so I thought I better ask the manager for it . . . *trails off*

Me: Right – I understand. *makes an understanding face* But maybe I can help? Are you after a gift for someone?

Deceptive Kind-Face: *purses lips* It's actually for a friend of mine – I want to get her a book – she lost her son six months ago and I want to get her something that might, like, help with the grief . . .

Me: Oh, god, I'm so sorry to hear that –

Deceptive Kind-Face: *starts to squirm impatiently* Yeah – I mean, he wasn't young – he was, like, 23 –

Me: *still feeling very sorry* Your friend must be devastated.

Deceptive Kind-Face: Yeah, she's *really* upset still. *raises eyebrows*

Me: *slightly baffled by the tone* So, ah, what kind of thing do you think would help?

Deceptive Kind-Face: Oh, just something on grief. *increasingly impatient* Something that'll help her move on!

Me: *changing gears rapidly* Are you guys close?

Deceptive Kind-Face: What?

Me: Are you close friends? I'm sorry to ask – I'm just trying to get an idea of what might be right for this – it's a very sensitive thing, choosing a book for something like this, and I want to give you some decent suggestions.

Deceptive Kind-Face: Oh, I mean, we're not *that* close – she works for me.

Me: *a horrible suspicion bubbles up; quickly forced back down* Okay. So I have a few things to suggest – there are a number of very beautiful memoirs on grief, or we've got some poetry collections which might be right . . . *comes out from behind the counter*

Deceptive Kind-Face: *tightens jaw; looks annoyed* Do you have something that will just *help*?

Me: *blinking* Ah, maybe – I'm not sure – I think sometimes reading about other people's grief helps –

Deceptive Kind-Face: What about, like, a gift book or something? Something small that'll just help her, like, move on!

Me: *suspicion reflux* Right – let me think for a moment – I'm having trouble getting a sense of what might be appropriate.

Deceptive Kind-Face: *looks annoyed; checks phone*

Me: *breathes in* So what were you hoping for with the book?

Deceptive Kind-Face: What?

Me: I guess what I'm wondering is what effect you're hoping for with the book – what do you want it to do?

Deceptive Kind-Face: *looks nonplussed* I want her to get over it. I mean, it's been a while, and she's still, like, over the top about it! *makes a knowing face* I think she's wallowing in it – it doesn't seem healthy.

Me: *reads this back* So you want a book that will speed up the process of your employee's grief for her son who died six months ago?

Deceptive Kind-Face: Yeah, just something small – is there a book like that?

Me: *face goes dead* No, I don't think there is a book like that. I really can't think of anything.

Deceptive Kind-Face: Do you think it's worth asking your manager?

88

Short, cheery, bandy-legged cockney dad and three sons, all in flat caps, rollick into the shop like a set of Bob Hoskins babushka dolls.

Cheery Flat Cap Cockney Dad: 'Allo, mate! Do you 'ave enny Terry Pra-chit then? I'm just gettin' George here on to 'im. *nods at George here*

Me: *delighted* Yes!

Rollick is the collective noun for cockneys.

A ROLLICK OF COCKNEYS

89

Cheery, fresh-faced man in a hoody marked with the corporate logo of a major internet investment and development company, signalling that he is or longs to be a Silicon Valley dongle: Hi mate! Do you have *Goodnight Moon?*

Me: Hi! Let me check . . . No, sorry – we just ran out.

Cheery Dongle: No worries! *browses around and returns with other baby books; watches on as I ring them up* How's business, anyway?

Me: *smiles; suddenly hates him* It's actually fine at the moment! It's our last flush before Amazon lands domestically and turns us into a smoking ruin. *twinkles*

Cheery Dongle: Yeah, sure – you guys will be okay, though – you do wrapping and stuff –

Me: *taking his money* Oh, for sure – and we have to hope that the local parts of what we do count for something. But that really depends –

Cheery Dongle: *smiles cheerily* You'll be alright!

Me: *continues sadistically* – depends on how far Amazon are able to drive down labour costs here, and how much they're willing to lose on the stock – loss leaders, that kind of thing – and given the pliancy of the government at the moment, it's not looking good.

Cheery Dongle: *senses the ideological challenge* Well, I suppose it's a matter of how much more expensive things are here – people might pay 20 per cent more for your books, but probably not 50 per cent –

Me: *ploughs through* Our margins are slim as it is, so a 10 to 20 per cent hit will probably send us off, or seriously hurt us – and given the way Amazon does business, I think it'll probably be much worse. I'm not optimistic about it, *bags up Dongle's books* but hey! Our gift-wrapping is pretty good, right? *twinkles, hands over books* Are you sorry you asked yet?

Cheery Dongle: *laughs nervously* Well, best of luck with everything!

Me: *smiles* And the same to you.

90

Friday, 2.25 p.m.

Me: **scans book placed on counter in post-lunch daze; brain activity reduced to muddy trickle after gruelling week of thesis writing; smiles offhandedly at pleasant older lady customer** $29.99.

Susan the Regular, unrecognisable with a gleaming new set of false teeth: **beams** Hello! Lovely to see you! How's the PhD?

Me: **caught flat-footed not recognising Susan the Regular because of disco-ball bright new snappers** Oh, Susan! Sorry! I didn't recognise you with your new **EMERGENCY CUSTOMER SERVICE SYSTEMS ACTIVATED – IMPENDING REFERENCE TO POTENTIALLY AWKWARD DENTAL PROSTHESIS – TAKING CONTROL OF SPEECH, COGNITION, AND MOTOR FUNCTIONS – SCANNING FOR ALTERNATIVE SAFE PHYSICAL REFERENTS ... FOUND. LAUNCHING ALTERNATIVE** haircut! It's shorter, isn't it? Looks great!

Susan the Regular: **beams again** Oh, thank you! It was a bit of a shock at first.

Me: *wildly relieved* Probably feels refreshing! *twinkles*

Susan the Regular: *delighted* It does! I've been on a bit of a spree – I got new glasses, a new haircut, and I even got new teeth. *bares her mithril gnashers*

Me: *like a worm* Did you? Wow!

91

Saturday, 11.45 a.m.

Sabre-toothed ragemum with three orbiting grotty eight- to eleven-year-old boys comes shouting through the shop to the children's section where I'm haplessly shelving like a giant ground sloth at a waterhole.

Sabre-Toothed Ragemum: Where are the *Percy Jackson* books?

Me: *blinks herbivorously* Just here. *taps shelf almost directly in front of where we're standing; Ragemum and Grotty Boys pile in, pushing me out of the way*

Sabre-Toothed Ragemum: Which one's the fifth one?

Me: *about to answer when one or more of the Grotty Boys farts quietly but weightily, a sighing exhalation of substantial duration and cubic volume* Hoh. *closes mouth; shuffles backwards out of smellcloud*

Sabre-Toothed Ragemum: *shuffles forwards, followed by Grotty Boys and cloud of stench* Which one is it?

Me: *clears nose in attempt to preserve soft palate* Hohhh – one sec. *shuffles backwards out of potent miasma*

Sabre-Toothed Ragemum: *shuffles forwards, with Grotty Boys and cloud, clearly annoyed* Do you have something else you'd rather be doing?!

Me: Oh, haha, no – sorry – I, ah *blinking through stench* – one of the boys just farted and I'm trying to stay clear of the smell.

Sabre-Toothed Ragemum: *livid* AW, JESUS, MAX! I TOLD YOU NOT TO DO ANY FARTS IN HERE!

Max: *outraged; in a high, strangled voice* AW, FAR OUT, MUM! I COULDN'T HELP IT!

Me: *loses it completely; cries with laughter*

92

Hard-eyed older woman in gym gear chewing an invisible cigar: Do you have *The Night Before Christmas*?

Me: *turns briefly from the customer he's mid-conversation with* You'll have to wait just a moment until I'm finished here.

Invisible Cigar: *seethes; replaces invisible cigar with actual enormous sushi roll and bites it*

Me: *finishes up with other customer* So, *The Night Before Christmas* . . . We don't have it at the moment –

Invisible Cigar: *gives me the full-force Helen Garner fuck-you-young-person-you're-probably-lying-and/or-a-murderer face* Do you have *any* Christmas books?

Me: *flinches under the impact of the Garner face* Not yet, no – it's early November, so we should be getting some soon.

Invisible Cigar: *with extraordinary severity and a remarkable amount of seaweed in her bottom teeth* When *will* you be getting them?

184

Me: *with provoking vagueness, running a hand through his hair*
Oh, I'm not sure – perhaps three weeks?

Invisible Cigar: *seethes predictably* You're very rude.

Me: *goes full Jeeves* Oh, I'm sorry to hear that. How's your sushi?

Invisible Cigar: *gathers herself; prepares to unleash hell*

Me: *turns his back and walks away*

93

Strange, tanned, woollen creature from shallowest, lightest California: Hiiiiiii! *smiles a smile as long and luxurious as the 'Palo Alto' playlist on Spotify*

Me: *braces for the cray* Hi! How can I help?

Woollen California: I see you have those – what are they? Mugs? With letters on the side?

Me: We do!

Woollen California: *scrunches up her face and pauses (probably) to twirl the silver rings on her toes by wriggling her feet in her sandals* Yeah!

Me: *blinks kindly and waits*

Woollen California: *stretches her arm up over her head and makes a contented sound* So do you have other letters?

Me: Ah, no, sorry, we've only got the challenging ones left – the ones with the high letter scores, like Q.

Woollen California: *bemused* Oh. I need T.

Me: We don't have T, I'm afraid – just Y, I, and Q.

Woollen California: Hmmm. *makes pantomime thinking face* It's for a Tom . . . I *guess* Q is kind of like a T? What do you think?

Me: Do I think Q is like T?

Woollen California: *brightly* Yeah!

Me: *wrestles briefly with conscience* No. Not really. Sorry.

Woollen California: Oh, no problem! *leaves merrily*

Me: *braces self against shelves for a moment*

94

Sunday, 10.50 a.m.

Wild-eyed little boy puts a book called *SHARKS!* on the counter.

Me: Just this one?

Shark Boy: Yes, please – it is about SHARKS and they are my favourites! *glares maniacally*

Me: *holding down laughter* Are they? What's your favourite shark?

Shark Boy: *goes full Ahab* My favourite is MEGALODON IT IS THE BIGGEST SHARK AND NOBODY HAS EVER SEEN IT OR KNOWS WHO IT IS! *stands in staring, silent rapture as visions of this mighty fish swim before his eyes*

Me: *tears of held-in laughter*

95

Monday, 4.55 p.m.

Eldritch British woman, apropos of nothing at all: A 70-year-old man?

Me, behind the counter, some distance away: *catches this wad of a question and begins interpretive origami* What does he normally read? Fiction, or non-fiction, or both?

Eldritch British Woman: *looks at me as into a glass darkly* . . . A card.

Me: *holds fast to his reason* Birthday cards are on the left – other cards on the right.

Eldritch British Woman: . . . Which will it be?

Me: *holds faster* Is it his birthday?

Eldritch British Woman: *browses cards like Professor Trelawney examining a takeaway menu* . . . Yes.

Me: What about this one? *holds up a Punch cartoon birthday card*

Eldritch British Woman: *inscrutably* Fine. It will go with this. *puts a book in my hand*

Me: *dazed* It will. Would you like me to wrap it for you?

Eldritch British Woman: *recoils slightly, peers deeply into the air in front of my face* . . . In what?

Me: *reels internally* . . . In paper. As a present. With a ribbon.

Eldritch British Woman: *wets her lips and looks sly* . . . Yes. That would be good.

Me: *wordlessly wraps book* There we are! All done. *tries a wavering smile*

Eldritch British Woman: *cocks head to the side, eyes gleaming* You enjoyed that, didn't you?

Me: *takes a white-knuckled mental grip on himself* Always a pleasure to help – have a good afternoon!

Eldritch British Woman: *leaves without a word*

Me: *breathes out; sags against counter*

96

Sunday, 2 p.m.

Cool indie couple around my age with media industry haircuts and really tasteful tattoos browsing the travel section pause their pleasant chat and take in the opening bars of 'Float On' by Modest Mouse playing on the shop Spotify.

Lady Indie, with a blonde topknot and money in her voice like Daisy Buchanan: Oh, man, this song is *old* now! You remember when we worked at General Pants?

Lord Indie, with a smooth, clever face and frames to match: Oh, man, that job was the worst – like, the *worst* . . . *relieved sigh-laugh*￼ Fuck, I'm glad I don't work in retail anymore.

Lady Indie: *sportively*￼ So do you think the 'kids' are into this song now as, like, a nostalgia property?

Lord Indie: *chuckles comfortably*￼ Or maybe *someone* still works in retail?

Both pause as Modest Mouse switches to Vampire Weekend.

LORD AND
LADY INDIE

Lady indie: *laughs* Maybe there's, like, a playlist on Spotify? 'I Still Work Here', or like . . .

Lord Indie: *taking up the joke* 'Too Old for This Shit'; 'I Had Dreams'; *puts on mock tone of officious bustle* 'Someone Had to Manage This Place When You All Left'.

Both chuckle.

Me, shelving gift books one bay over, out of their line of sight: *staggers to the counter, changes the music, then expires like Boromir, pierced with cruel shafts*

97

Incredibly patient mum trailing after a grabby little snivel-wretch: Xavier, if you touch anything else, we're leaving.

Xavier, the grabby little snivelwretch: *pulls a hideously impudent face and knocks over a box set on purpose*

Incredibly patient mum: *snaps; latches on to snivelwretch's wrist, drags him round to face her, and delivers the following through clenched teeth with a kind of white-hot restrained rage* Xavier, if you touch ANYTHING ELSE in here, I'll tie you up outside like a DOG!

Xavier, the grabby little snivelwretch: *awed silence*

98

Thursday, 3.40 p.m.

Me: *answers phone on the fourth ring* North Sh–

Intermittent shouter who sounds almost as much as, it turns out, she looks like Amanda Vanstone: *cuts right across my greeting in a sardonic, aggrieved tone, as if I were a waiter who'd been ignoring her hand in the air* HELLO?! FINALLY! Do you have Bill Leak's book? It was advertised in *The Australian* and I WANT IT FOR CHRISTMAS!

Me: *swallows the rudeness* Which one were you after?

Sounds like Vanstone (SLV): *sardonically* Well, how many ARE THERE?!

Me: *coolly* There are three. I assume you're after the latest one. We've got one left – would you like me to put it aside for you?

SLV: *sceptically* Are you SURE? I don't want to make the trip for NO REASON!

Me: *curtly* I have it in my hand – I'll put it on hold for you.

SLV: *hangs up*

Me: *sighs through his teeth, puts the phone down and the book in the holds cupboard*

Fifteen minutes later, SLV marches in with a set jaw, looking remarkably like Amanda Vanstone.

Me: *identifies SLV by sight; retrieves Leak from the cupboard* Hi! Were you after the Bill Leak?

SLV: *takes me in with a bulging eye* How much is it?

Me: $45

SLV: CHRIST! That MUCH? You're JOKING!

Me: *clouds over around the brow*

SLV: *sighs; opens purse; licks fingers* Probably not even worth asking if you take American Express –

Me: *calmly* We do.

SLV: But you probably put a BLOODY SURCHARGE on it! How much is that gonna cost me?

Me: *painfully aware of the line building behind SLV* We don't –

SLV: *cuts me off* It's OUTRAGEOUS the surcharge you retailers put on American Express! We're usually very good customers and YOU'D THINK –

Me: *very keen to hurry her on* There's no surcharge –

SLV: *ploughs on* I don't see how you can TURN MONEY AWAY! I pay ENOUGH ON FEES –

Me: *one eye on the growing line, one ear on the now-ringing phone* We don't –

SLV: And FOR-tee FIVE DOLLars is-

Me: *loses his temper; drops an octave; booms from the chest* STOP SPEAKING AND LISTEN TO WHAT I'M TELLING YOU: THERE IS NO SURCHARGE ON AMERICAN EXPRESS.

SLV: *stunned silence*

Me: *breathes out; a colleague answers the phone in the back office* That's $45, thanks. You can tap on the side. *gestures at the payWave sensor*

SLV: *taps her card*

Me: *bags the book* Thank you.

SLV: *takes her bag* Thank you. *leaves the store*

Me: *steadies himself; smiles at the line of customers* Who was next?

Woman talking on her phone lumps grocery shopping on counter, squashing the gift books: *breaks off phone conversation* I'll ask him – *to me* hi, do you price-match?

99

Monday, 5.20 p.m.

Woman with asymmetrical fringe and black-rimmed glasses as thick as her Eastern European accent: Do yo hyev Ghaffka Myetomorrphosys book?

Me: *buffers* . . . *delighted* Yes!

100

Sunday, 11 a.m.

Abstracted woman in gym gear puts card on the counter, taps it, and browses the counter gift books.

Me: So just the card?

Abstract Tapper: *browsing* . . . Mmm.

Me: $6.95

Abstract Tapper: . . . *mutely, and without any eye contact, presents a $20 note*

Me: *takes the note* Would you like a little bag?

Abstract Tapper: *still browsing* . . .

Me: *suppresses a sigh* Bag?

Abstract Tapper: *again without eye contact* . . . No.

Me: *processes transaction, places change and receipt next to card on counter, and walks away*

Abstract Tapper: *after a good 30 seconds* Excuse me!

Me: *spins* Yes?

Abstract Tapper: Don't just walk away from me! Where's my change?!

Me: *mood passes through several Shakespearean villains before settling, with an inaudible groan, into Macbeth, Act V, 'the sere, the yellow leaf'* On the counter in front of you, with your card and receipt.

Abstract Tapper: *makes a wonderful show of discovering card, change, etc.* Oh! Well, can I at least have a *bag*?

Me: *smiiiiles* Of course!

101

Saturday, 10.30 a.m.

Elderly British gentleman with neat socks, anorak, and notice-ably puckered lips shuffles towards the counter after poisoning a passing trolley-pushing woman with his patrician eye.

Old Pucker: Good morning! *eyes me trepidatiously; wets lips* I hope you can help me.

Me: *with subalternly briskness* Good morning! So do I! How can I help?

Old Pucker: I'm looking for titles concerning Bwritish wrail-ways in India – a vehry dear friend of mine is terwibly intewrested in them, *pauses to refresh lips* and I feel certain I heard a pahticular book mentioned . . . Oh, where was it?

Me: *heroically conceals amusement* I think I know the book you're after – is it a hardback with pictures?

Old Pucker: *heartily pleased* Yehs! The very one! *licks lips with great satisfaction*

Me: *breathes in very slowly and carefully* Ah – hahaha – ahem. Great. Let me – ahaha – let me just see if we still have it in stock for you – won't be a moment. *checks the computer*

Old Pucker: Hmm. *eyes roam; latch on to the fancy fountainpen display near the till* My goodness! A wreal pen!

Me: Oh? Yeah, they're nice, aren't they?

Old Pucker: *wets lips* Do you know, in my opinion, *everwyone* should have to use a pen with a nib – a wreal pen – not those dwreadful biwos! We should go back to teaching evewry child to write with ink.

Me: *still fighting down laughter* Oh, I don't know – biros have their advantages. Fountain pens can be very messy – my dad tells horrible stories of drinking the school ink to frighten his teacher.

Old Pucker: *twitches eyebrows compulsively; wets lips and half-opens them* Ohoho – do you know, do you know, *takes two sharp breaths in preparation for drollery* I used to use mine to poison my mother's aspidistra –

OLD PUCKER

Me: *loses it completely; howls with laughter; thumps counter; doubles over*

Old Pucker: *pinkens; twinkles; pleased with enthusiastic reception of this excellent prank*

102

Christmas Eve, 8.45 a.m.

Quarter to nine – fifteen minutes to open – on Christmas Eve, biggest day of the year. Staff frantically preparing the shop. Mule-faced lady pulls up outside with a massive trolley, bangs impatiently on the glass doors.

Muleface: *through the closed door* What time do you open?

My Colleague Arthur (MCA): Nine o'clock!

Muleface: FUCK YOU! *leaves with her trolley*

MCA: Merry Christmas!

103

Bald pink man with the sour face of someone who quibbles over portion sizes at the RSL dumps book on counter; glowers.

Me: *smiles* So just that one?

Sour Bald Pinky: *continues to glower*

Me: *heartily* Right you are, then! *scans the book* $29.99.

Sour Bald Pinky: *glowers; presents credit card*

Me: Shall I just tap it? *raises brows like helpful kelpie*

Sour Bald Pinky: *scowls*

Me: *grins delightedly* I'll take that as a yes! *taps the card*

Sour Bald Pinky: *returns to first position glower*

Me: *bundles receipt and book up just out of Sour Bald Pinky's reach* Would you like a bag?

Sour Bald Pinky: *scowls*

Me: *helpful kelpie*

Sour Bald Pinky: *scowls*

Me: *kelpie*

Sour Bald Pinky: *scowls*

Me: *kelpie*

Sour Bald Pinky: *scowls*

Me: *kelpie*

Sour Bald Pinky: *finally; grudgingly; like a boy apologising to his sister* . . . If you've got one.

Me: *with sadistic glee* Would you like a paper bag or a plastic bag?

104

Supercool chill guy called Spencer shopping for his bro's new baby: Hey, thanks for your help, m'man – I'm-a get this for the little one. *spins picture book across the counter as only a supercool chill guy named Spencer would* And can you wrap it, bro? *checks his phone*

Me: *bro-induced ice forms over his heart* Sure. What colour would suit the little one?

Superchill Spencer: *distracted, with his mouth open* Hay?

Me: *carefully* Is it a boy or a girl or doesn't matter?

Superchill Spencer: *passionately* Orr, like, as if that even *matters*, bro – it's 2018!

Me: *quickly* Oh no, for sure, I couldn't agree more – but people get weird about babies. I've had to rewrap stuff –

Superchill Spencer: *outraged* Orr, fuck, *seriously?* Like, it should just be any colour that's *thinks* COLOURFUL! *laughs delightedly at his insight* Man, you shouldn't even ask 'em, ay – just like, what you pick they get. Boom! *chuckles*

Me: *grins* Alright, then. *pulls out the pinkest paper he has*

Superchill Spencer: *baulks* Orr. Maybe not pink, but, hay?

* * *

Five minutes later, wealthy blonde Brexit refugee who pro-
nounces 'book' as 'berk', after sighing passive-aggressively
over our lack of berks about moving to Dubai as her friends
recently did, settles on a pair of luridly pink berks for their
daughter.

Brexit Refugee: What a pity. I was really hoping you could
    help me . . . *sighs again* I suppose I'll just take these,
    please, and *with no hint of a question* would you mind
    wrapping them. *looks away before I answer; checks her phone*

Me: No worries. Is purple okay?

Brexit Refugee: *not paying attention, eyes on screen* . . . Hmm?
    Oh, fine – whatever, really.

Me: *wraps berks; selects gold ribbon to go with purple*

Brexit Refugee: *instantly* Actually, do you have anything other than gold? It's not really good for children? It's a bit old lady, don't you think?

Me: *blinks in a dignified, owlish way; has never been so insulted in all his life* Of course. What about pink?

Brexit Refugee: *loses interest as I start to comply* Yeah, that's fine. *goes back to her phone*

105

Saturday, 9.50 a.m.

Little boy in a stroller, watching on as his mum browses the fiction section, in a high, sweet voice, mournfully, and with extraordinary dignity, sings: Fruuuuiiiit saaalaad . . . yummy . . . yummy . . .

106

Sunday, 10.45 a.m.

Pompous regular who looks like a paunchy Richard Glover, and whose incredible sensitivity to even the slightest hint of condescension is only outmatched by his total inability to understand basic facts or manage simple comprehension tasks leans on the counter.

Paunchy Glover: *haughtily* So what are you telling me? You can't get it for me?

Me: *with* The Hurt Locker *levels of focus and delicacy* No, the problem is that the musician in question hasn't released a new memoir, and his previous memoir is out of print.

Paunchy Glover: *Glover senses tingling* So you're saying I'm wrong then?

Me: No, no – he certainly did write a memoir, but I'm afraid it's out of print. It's about ten years old.

Pauncy Glover: *with a triumphant drawing in of breath through the nostrils* So why is it in the paper then? *stabs finger into scrap of* Spectrum *he's brought in as evidence*

Me: *explains it again as if for the first time* Well, he's released a new album that extends on work he did in the memoir – they're songs inspired by the memoir. *subtly turns the scrap of newsprint back towards Paunchy Glover for easier reading and comprehension*

Paunchy Glover: *suspiciously* How do you know that?

Me: *restrains frustration at great personal cost* You'll see down the side of the column it says 'Album Review', and it covers the memoir in the review, *smiles benignly; continues on cat paws* which is probably where the trouble started.

Paunchy Glover: *knows he is defeated; launches final gambit* So do you have the album?

Me: *gives his best shopman's laugh* Ha ha! No. If only. We could sell them together, as a package deal.

Paunchy Glover: *senses an opening* So why don't you? I could probably get them both on Amazon.

Me: *redirects the force* And why not? Since we can't source either for you, you can do it with a clean conscience. *smiles*

214

Paunchy Glover: *maddened by this* Probably save me a lot of time, too. *spitefully* Amazon are opening in Australia soon, aren't they? How will you handle that kind of competition?

Me: *pretends question is in good faith and shifts gears to sombre concern for future* Well, it'll be difficult – we're not a massive multinational with the luxury of making a loss for years to drive smaller operations out of business – we'll have to see how it goes, and if we have a loyal enough customer base.

Paunchy Glover: *snorts* And what if you don't?

Me: *smiles with teeth* Then you and I will have to find something else to do with our Sunday mornings. *leaves counter*

Paunchy Glover: *suddenly vulnerable* Thanks for your help!

Me: *over his shoulder on the way to the shelving shelf* No worries, have a good one!

107

Big, florid, deep-voiced man with his polo shirt tucked into his jeans: *lugubriously* Do you have Mark Latham's new book, *Outsiders?*

Me: *delighted* No!

108

Too-busy Ita Buttrose type, dripping in gold like a Celtic priestess with a real estate business: *sniffily adjusts her scarf* Yes, you've had a book in for me. *turns away to signal she is a woman of consequence and is very busy*

Me: *enjoys the syntax* Of course. What's your last name?

Too-Busy Buttrose: *haughtily, assuming I mean the author's last name* Oh, I don't recall. Can't you just look up *my* name?

Me: *smiles; repeats* Of course. What's your last name?

Too-Busy Buttrose: Alice. *adjusts scarf*

Me: *gingerly* So your last name is Alice?

Too-Busy Buttrose: *severely* Yes!

Me: *pretty certain Alice is her first name; checks on-hold cupboard anyway* That's odd – it doesn't seem to be here.

Too-Busy Buttrose: Well, I don't see how that can be! Someone contacted me yesterday. *droops her mouth and raises her eyebrows in a 'what-kind-of-show-are-you-running-here?' expression*

Me: *in a bind, unable to contradict Too-Busy Buttrose without further provoking her; tries a new tack* And is your last name spelled A-L-I-C-E?

Too-Busy Buttrose: *more exasperated* Yes!

Me: *has a blinding flash of genius* Of course. And what's your first name?

Too-Busy Buttrose: *impatiently* Alice!

Me: *smiles triumphantly* I see – and so what's your last name?

Too-Busy Buttrose: *angrily, with absolutely no sense of her absurdity* Lacroix! L. A. C. R. O. I. X!

Me: *smiles; fetches book* There we are! We got there in the end!

Too-Busy Buttrose: *shakes her head incredulously* My goodness! At last. That was very hard work! I think you need to organise yourselves a little better, don't you?

Me: *smiles* Oh yes. *fatuously* Always.

109

Sunday, 4.55 p.m.

At the supermarket after work using the automated checkout, I recognise and avoid the eye of an incredibly painful regular customer at the bookshop, true proficient in the art of aggrieved helplessness.

Painful Regular: *snorts, taps screen with growing impatience* Come on, COME on! STUPID machine!

Me: *scans purchases faster*

Painful Regular: *to my half-turned shoulder* Hey, you work here! How do I fix this STUPID machine?

Me: *turns to look at Painful Regular* I don't work here. *finishes his stack of groceries and pays*

Painful Regular: Yes you do! I know your face.

Me: *puts stuff in backpack* I work in the bookshop.

Painful Regular: *delighted* Oh yeeeaaah! That's right! Do you know how to fix this machine?

Me: *hesitates* I . . . do. *sighs* See how it says on the screen: 'Scan first item to begin'?

Painful Regular: Yeah?

Me: Do that – scan your first item.

Painful Regular: *does that* Oh! There it goes!

Me: *smiles thinly; leaves*

110

Sunday, 2.20 p.m.

Receiving reactionary filth [in my opinion] from New Holland Publishers in the back office with the door propped open, quietly loathing my job, when there's a soft knock on the door frame. I look up to see a teen girl standing in the doorway in sneakers, jeans and a plaid shirt, smiling apologetically – the Muse of Slackers, Schlubs, and Service Workers.

Me: *delighted to be pulled away from an invoice that includes the Mark Latham/Alan Jones cookbook* Hi! How can I help?

Muse of Slackers, Schlubs, and Service Workers (MSSSW): Hey – sorry – not important at all, but I'm just wondering what the playlist we're listening to is called. It's – *smiles and nods her head shyly* it's a really good time.

Me: *enjoys this a lot; pauses for a second to pay attention to the music, perfect shop indie with cruisy, chorus-rich strums and a luxuriously melancholic whale-song male vocal over the top* I'm not sure, let me check with my colleague – he put it on.

MSSSW: Oh, no, don't worry! It doesn't matter! *gestures I should sit back down*

Me: *twinkles* No, no – I want to know, too. It's good, isn't it? *slopes to the front counter and checks with younger colleague, writes down band and album name on a Post-it, then presents it to MSSSW*

MSSSW: *makes small bow* Thank you so much – do you mind if I hang out in here a bit longer? It's such a nice store.

Me: *smiles sadly, even more aware of his role in a comfortably derivative and powerfully sentimental vision of working in a bookshop/record store, a pocket universe of reverie and interlude where life leaves you alone –*

so shelter'd from annoy,

That I may never know how change the moons,

Or hear the voice of busy common-sense!

– and with a sense of being added as a character (The Bookseller, tall, paunchy, fluffy, balding, with tortoise-shell glasses, a penchant for plaid, and an air of wary sauropodal

THE BOOKSELLER

benignity) to the gorgeous, unownable, never-to-be-finished novel MSSSW is writing about herself* Of course. Take your time – enjoy! *returns to Jones and Latham*

111

Sunday, 3.55 p.m.

Old Lady with a mean rinse and a mouth like a bulldog clip, on her way out: All these books and I don't wanna read any of 'em!

Me: *smiles apologetically* Well, you'll have to write your own!

Meanrinse Clipmouth: *sourly, without missing a beat* Couldn't do worse than some of this rubbish! *gestures at whole shop*